Rethinking
COLLEGE

Rethinking
COLLEGE

A
GUIDE TO
THRIVING
WITHOUT
A DEGREE

KARIN KLEIN

HARPER HORIZON

ISBN: 978-1-4003-3448-3 (eBook)
ISBN: 978-1-4003-3447-6 (HC)

Library of Congress Control Number: 2024933380

Printed in the United States of America
24 25 26 27 28 LBC 5 4 3 2 1

For Talya, Sam, and Aviva
Who are always in the conversation

CONTENTS

INTRODUCTION

My parents were smart, well-read people. On Sunday mornings, our living room was strewn with the sections of the *New York Times* and other newspapers, and after breakfast, we all sat around reading them and trading them back and forth. My father liked to sit in the living room after work with a bowl of snacks to eat and a pile of books next to him, which he would devour on weekdays and return to the library on Saturday to borrow a new pile.

But neither Dad nor Mommy had gone to college. In fact, because he was supporting his parents and siblings during the Great Depression, Dad hadn't been able to finish high school.

Yet until he died in 2009, he would frequently call me on the phone to discuss the news he'd read in the *Times*: "Did you see this article on page A29 and this one on page C11?" I was a professional journalist, a college grad, and I'd been to grad school, but there was no way I could possibly keep up with the man.

He was a salesman, and his gregarious nature made him successful at it. Mommy was more reserved, naturally wise, and inclined to reflection. Both were independent, open-minded thinkers.

So from the start, and at the deepest level, the reality in my family was that formal education didn't necessarily have much to do with braininess, life success, or originality of thought. In my family's eyes, the intrinsic value of a person had little to do with the extrinsic value of his credentials or her bank account.

Yet my parents also revered the education they hadn't been able to get. And though they never pushed me about school or grades, they were thrilled when I was accepted to a prestigious college with a scholarship and when I chose journalism as my career, after all those Sunday mornings with the newspapers.

It's part of my culture, my upbringing, and my profession to question authority and trends that people swallow without really knowing much about them. My daily work as an opinion writer required me to look deeply and critically at current events.

For example, it's misleading for Americans to be told that eating a certain way will raise the risk of a certain cancer by 25 percent when what that means in some cases is the risk will go from 4 percent to 5 percent. And I was irritated no end by the environmental scientist who, completely without evidence, scared the public into thinking that they might inhale COVID-19 from ocean spray when walking along the beach.

As an education writer, I'd watched a lot of wild pendulum swings without seeing students learn a whole lot more.

The No Child Left Behind Act struck me as one of the worst-constructed laws ever seen.

So when Bill Gates announced a push to get far more high school students to attend four-year colleges, and the movement gained traction, I was highly skeptical, to say the least. Though I thought the Bill and Melinda Gates Foundation had done some good things in education, as a longtime education writer, I'd also seen notable failures. It dropped its initiatives to evaluate teachers based in large part on the standardized test scores of their students, and on funding smaller high schools, after studies found that neither idea worked well.

Suddenly, school districts were making all students pass the full slate of courses required to attend four-year colleges, with the grades required to attend, even when that had nothing to do with the students' plans, interests, or talents. No surprise, in the Los Angeles schools, far more students were heading toward not being able to get their diplomas until the school district dropped its grade requirements from C to D. This was not an educational improvement.

Much of this movement came from good intentions. Students of color and poverty had for too long been herded nearly automatically into vocational tracks, their ambitions curtailed before they could even get started. That needed fixing, but the solution that politicians and policy-makers came up with was a sledgehammer.

Schools were judged on how many kids they sent to college. Some were publicly posting students' plans for after high school. The hint was there: some were successes and some weren't. That's probably why, at Sheboygan South High School in Wisconsin, a hefty number of high school seniors were marking on a form that they were heading to college even when that wasn't actually their plan.

College has always held prestige in our society, but it was getting out of control. Not headed for a bachelor's degree? Then you were seen as second-rate, lacking in brainpower, and doomed to a mediocre life at best. Meanwhile, college grads with indeterminate skills and lack of clarity about their futures were shunted into jobs that had been performed perfectly well by high school grads.

That, in turn, led employers to start demanding college degrees for jobs that had never required them before, a phenomenon known as degree inflation. Meanwhile, the tremendous potential of people whose natural talents lay outside the classroom was going to waste.

Surely I wasn't the only person who thought the whole system was messed up.

Then I heard about how things are done in Switzerland, where people with different talents and goals are given a fitting and respectful education that gets them started on the life they want, not the life some politician or education reformer has decided they should want. There are people trying to do something similar here. You'll read about all this in the book.

Americans are in revolt right now, ready to say that not everybody wants or needs to attend a four-year college. But they're missing something: information about what else they might do, how they might get started on a good life. School counselors have a limited bag of options to offer them. And that's where this book comes in.

Though I am specifically reaching out to high school students and their families, this book also will help college students who wonder: What's next? Too many wander through their college years looking for the inspiration that will guide them to the right major and their future careers. That's how they end up underemployed, unfulfilled, and, for too many, mired in debt. The paths in this book, and the specific information on how to get started on them, will work for the college educated as well.

It would be even better if this book helped revolutionize the school counseling profession so that students are exposed to far more helpful information about the possibilities for their futures.

And finally, it's my hope that all Americans, when they see something inappropriate going on, will stand up and shout about it.

A NOTE ON
HOW TO READ
THIS BOOK

It surprised even me, during the research and interviewing for this book, how many people fit into multiple categories covered in this book. Many creative people have their own businesses and thus are entrepreneurs. But then, so are former military personnel.

Those same people often work their way up from the bottom, the topic of another chapter. And many apprentices are working for companies that have shown openness to hiring people without a four-year degree, though those are two separate chapters. Those who look to work overseas often choose outdoor work, and some of those people are doing volunteer work. People don't fit neatly into single categories for the most part, which is a great thing.

In other words, it would help you the most not to pick and choose chapters too much. Yes, you may have zero interest in the military or the skilled trades, so skipping those chapters would make sense for you. (Unless, maybe, you'd never realized you could learn to be an animal handler in the military?) But it's likely you'll find helpful information and examples on creative people in more chapters than the one specifically on creative work.

The more chapters you read, the more you'll find surprising avenues for your future and inspiring people who offered their time and stories in interviews in order to help you along the way. Listen to them.

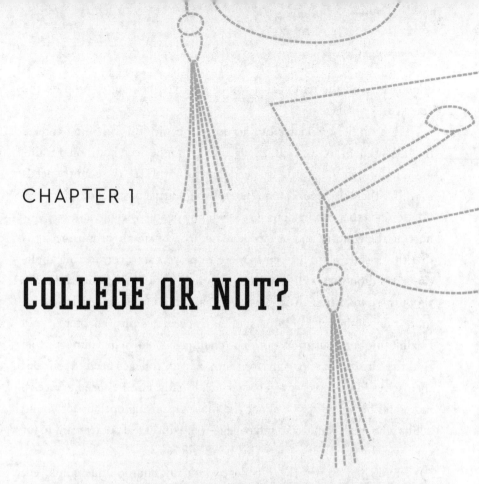

CHAPTER 1

COLLEGE OR NOT?

There's a big disconnect in America. For years, we've been hearing about the importance of a college degree. It's been drummed into us that a college education is practically a prerequisite for the jobs of the twenty-first century. We've been warned that other countries will knock us out of the global economy unless more and more of our students earn four-year degrees.

What we hear less of is that not everyone *wants* a college education, or is ready for it, or is prepared to succeed at it, or knows what to do with it. Many countries do a much better job of preparing teenagers for well-paid jobs—including white-collar, management-level jobs—without four-year degrees.

The time is ripe for change. It's becoming clear that not everyone needs a four-year college degree or is better off with one. The insistence on a college degree as a job requirement is harming employers, employees, and the nation as a whole. It's even helping to prop up the crazy cost of college.

High school graduates can go on to meaningful, fulfilling careers that allow them to live well, though many might need additional training. But for that to happen, we need four things: First, the country needs to realize that "degree inflation"—requiring formal postsecondary education for jobs that can be done just as well by people without a degree—is hurting the country and has to be remedied. There are promising signs that this is starting to happen as more employers start considering applicants based on their skills, not their degrees. (You'll find out a lot more about these in chapter 10.) Second, we as a nation need to develop other, more robust alternative paths such as apprenticeships (chapter 4) and flexible higher-education options (chapter 12) to help young people find the futures that are right for them. Third, colleges need to reinvent themselves in multiple ways (chapter 12). Finally, families need to receive more and better guidance about the most promising options for young adults who don't want to attend college—or who at least don't want to (or can't) right now. That's where this book comes in.

More than 40 percent of college graduates end up underemployed, working in jobs that don't require a bachelor's degree, according to "10 Facts about Today's College Graduates" by Katherine Schaeffer at Pew Research Center.[1]

And that sort of thing happens after many graduates have taken on debt to pay for a prohibitively expensive education that can retail for more than $80,000 a year in some cases, which is what my alma mater Wellesley College charges—the fee for the full academic year of 2023-24 was $83,920. When I entered college in 1971, it cost $3,400 a year—which, in today's prices, would translate to a little more than $25,000 if the price had simply gone up at the rate of inflation. That's far less than the retail price for a private college now. No wonder only half of Americans think the benefits of a college education outweigh the cost, according to Public Agenda.[2]

Plus, of those who enroll in public four-year colleges, more than 30 percent don't attain a degree, even within six years. They carry the debt of college grads without the potential boost in earning power to help them pay back student loans.

These are the students who at least try college. Close to 40 percent of young people never do, according to the US Bureau of Labor Statistics. Clearly, college is not the path to success for many, many people. And yet, beyond directing them to the military or the manual trades—both valid paths but not right for everyone—schools give them little guidance on the options for moving forward in life.

We fail in this regard even though college is less and less of an attraction to young Americans. A Gallup survey found that in 2013, 74 percent of adults ages 18–29 thought a college education was "very important." By 2019, the number had plummeted to 41 percent.[3]

Yet while our society frets about the overwrought efforts by a few students to gain admission to prestigious colleges—with book after book written on how to impress the admissions officers at schools like Stanford—scant attention is paid to helping the people whose interests and talents lie outside the conventional college path.

The college dream has been pushed so hard that there are no comprehensive guides or resource books for young people (or their parents) seeking practical information about alternatives to a conventional four-year college degree. Until now.

In case you thought a bachelor's degree was a necessity, consider this: according to a Georgetown University study, nearly 30 percent of people with a two-year associate's degree from a community college earn more than the average holder of a four-year degree.

Clearly, there's plenty of room for success among those who don't aim for a bachelor's degree.

I was raised in a different time, when a college education wasn't expected or required for many jobs. Still, my parents raised me to revere education, especially my father, who had been forced to drop out of high school to help support his parents and siblings during the Great Depression. Though he was a successful salesman—and avid reader, who chowed down on a pile of library books every week—he had huge respect for highly educated people and a sense of shame about his lack of formal education. When I, his youngest child, received a scholarship to attend Wellesley College, he was literally in tears that our family had made this jump in one generation.

So don't get me wrong: this is by no means an anticollege book. I'm a college graduate and a big believer in education, though now there are many ways to become and stay an educated person. For me, college was the right place to go. I've always felt comfortable in classes and have recently gone back to school part-time. My career as an editorial writer for the *Los Angeles Times* has been, in a way, like a continuation of college: researching and writing persuasive essays for a living. And I support efforts to make college education more accessible to students of color and more affordable by all.

That said, my beef with the current system is this: too many young people are going off to institutions of higher learning mainly because they think that's what you do after high school. They do it even when they have little idea why they're applying, if they can afford it, whether they're prepared and truly interested, what they seek to accomplish there, and whether there are other, equally valid paths for them. Others know they don't want college but are pressured by school counselors, peers, and society at large.

High schools and most colleges cater to—actually, they demand—a certain narrow band of intelligence. People whose tremendous talents lie outside that band are made to feel like failures. Among the people you'll meet in this book is a sound editor who has worked on many of the biggest films for many of the biggest directors and has become a very wealthy man. He has dyslexia, so he tended to learn by sound, which became a hugely important element of his life starting at a young age.

College is not just expensive, but young people are also using four-plus years of their lives that might have been better spent exploring the world and their interests, building the start of their career, and getting some money in the bank.

When the title of this book mentions "rethinking college," it's about more than creating a great life without college. It could mean finding the time in life that's right for attending college or deciding how much college is right for you—and that itself might change as you feel inspired to seek out new knowledge or skills. It certainly should mean that colleges should rethink themselves. Why can't four-year colleges also be two-year colleges, granting associate's degrees to students who find they can't or don't want to go all the way to a bachelor's? Or giving students who don't finish their degrees broad latitude in how they might do that later, through work experience or independent study or other means? The world is changing rapidly, but colleges have been slow to respond.

•

Connie Chang followed a path considered a sure winner in our science-oriented society: she got her degree at Harvard University in biophysics, then went on to earn a PhD at Cornell University. By that time, she had been in postsecondary school for ten years. The educational requirements didn't stop there. Students like Connie were expected to follow up with two or three postdoctoral stints. Her ultimate goal was either to be a professor or perhaps do research in a federal laboratory.

But during Connie's first postdoc, a year and a half at Rutgers University, her adviser left partway through. That meant she didn't get to publish research papers, which is essential to getting more postdocs. And because she was married and her husband's job at the time required living in the New York area, she wasn't able to look elsewhere for academic opportunities. She switched to the finance world, and the couple eventually settled in the San Francisco Bay Area.

Outwardly, Connie has what most people would consider a dream job. She makes close to $200,000 a year testing credit-risk models for a bank, although she points out that in the Bay Area, with its ultrahigh housing and other costs, her salary doesn't buy a luxury lifestyle.

More important, though, Connie is less than thrilled with her career.

She's deeply thoughtful about what makes for good work in the current world.

"I'm not even middle management. I feel like I'm a cog in the machine," she said, adding that the job tends to be repetitive in nature and doesn't allow for much in the way of growth. "I could be replaced tomorrow. It's not what I pictured myself doing."

And yet, because of the many years she spent getting a higher education, she feels that now that she's in her midforties, the opportunities are narrowing.

"There's a huge premium put on youth in some of these places," she said. "I feel like I've aged out of changing fields. I can't switch now. I kind of feel stuck."

Her previous boss liked having employees with a doctorate. Now, she said, things have changed. The bank might prefer to hire someone with a decent knowledge of math who can learn to do data programming. "Part of me is concerned about being pushed out," she said.

In order to do the creative work she craves, Connie is a freelance writer—on top of having her full-time job and being the mother of two children. She started out writing about parenting issues and now does articles on biomedicine, writing for *National Geographic* and other publications. In order to fit it all in, she rises before her children do. Fortunately, she said, she doesn't need much sleep.

I asked Connie what she would think if one of her children chose to forgo the four-year-college route. She paused to think about it. All things being equal, she certainly wants them to get a college education. But . . .

"My experience shows you can have all the credentials in the world, and it won't necessarily get you life satisfaction," she said. "If they are willing to devote time and energy to what they love doing, that's what I'd want for them.

"I don't want them to fall into the trap of perpetually striving; I want them to be able to enjoy themselves. Hopefully they're contributing something. Doing something that they're passionate about and then getting financial stability.

"I want them to find someone to love who loves them and find work that they find meaning in that gets them excited to start each new day."

•

Like Connie, many college graduates end up working in fields largely unrelated to what they studied. Of course, students change their majors all the time—I didn't change mine, but I also never worked in a field remotely connected to it—and not everyone goes to college with a career foremost in their minds. Some attend to become greater thinkers and scholars, to learn history or religion or literature, not necessarily in order to get a well-paid job. That's a wonderful ambition, too, as long as they can afford it and have an idea of what they'll do afterward. There's nothing wrong with changing our minds during or after college, and it's actually a valuable skill to be able to turn from one career to another in a rapidly changing economy.

The problem occurs when young people choose to attend college only or primarily because that is expected of them after high school or because they believe it's impossible to accomplish great things without that bachelor's degree—or to party. College isn't the right choice just because you finished high school and have no idea where you fit in the real world. There are other rewarding and far less expensive ways to find your interests and carve out a future—which *then* might lead you to college. At that point, you will know more about yourself and what you want in your life, and how college fits in with that. You'll have a more mature and interesting résumé that will impress college admissions officers. And you might well be working for an organization that provides tuition reimbursement for higher education. The standard high-school-to-college pipeline is just that—standard. Automatic. Unnecessary for many people.

To paraphrase poet Mary Oliver: You get just one wild and precious life. What are you going to do with it? There's nothing inherently wrong with following a conventional path of high school to four-year college—unless it isn't what you're yearning to do. If you're doing it out of fear rather than desire, then it may not be the right choice for you.

Maybe you want to try some form of public service, learn how to train horses, work your way up in the corporate world, or make some money by going to a short-term coding camp and working in the tech industry. In this book, you'll meet a young woman who never misses an opportunity to be an entrepreneur, a man who became one of the first pilots in the nation to work for a major airline without a college degree, a makeup artist, an author, a woman who earned a bachelor's degree and then decided to become an electrician instead, and a manager arranging tours for musical performers. They're all people who were brave enough to take a different path in life. Some make a lot of money; some don't. But they have found meaning and satisfaction in the lives they are creating.

I want you to finish reading this book feeling inspired to explore the different ways in which you can begin shaping your own life. I will provide practical tools and information for career paths that are both *broad* and *specific*—from learning corporate management skills in the military to taking on an apprenticeship to finding opportunities to live and work abroad. You'll learn about a nontraditional college that costs less money and provides credit for active work, not just sitting in a classroom, and ways to use bottom-rung jobs to scaffold a career in a coveted field of work. And you will learn about them from the experiences of people who have done it and are doing it now.

Of the ten fastest-growing job categories in the nation, only *two*—nurse practitioners and statisticians—require college degrees, according to the U.S. Bureau of Labor Statistics. The others, which include cooks, athletes, and information security analysts, can enter their fields without a bachelor's degree.

Things are changing. It turns out that right now is the best time in decades for young people to thrive financially, intellectually, creatively, and emotionally without a bachelor's degree. Employers are more willing to look at life experiences that might have taught applicants skills and wisdom just as well as or even better than a formal education. The new mantra is "skills before degrees."

This new attitude has even reached into the office of the president of the United States. Former President Donald Trump signed an executive order in 2020 directing federal agencies to change their hiring policies to eliminate minimum education requirements, unless a degree was legally needed for a job, and focus on skills instead. At least eight states—Alaska, Colorado, Maryland, New Jersey, North Carolina, Pennsylvania, Utah, and Virginia—also have greatly reduced the number of state jobs requiring a four-year college education. In his 2023 State of the Union address, President Joe Biden joined the chorus for de-emphasizing degrees.

"Let's offer every American the path to a good career whether they go to college or not," Biden said, noting that outside Columbus, Ohio, Intel was building semiconductor factories that would create thousands of jobs, many of them paying $130,000 without requiring a degree.

Major employers are signing on to the skills-over-degrees concept. Half of the jobs at IBM don't require a bachelor's. Other large companies have joined the movement, including Accenture, Apple, Bank of America, General Motors, and Google.

After hearing through the years from smart, qualified people who couldn't land jobs because they lacked a bachelor's, I wrote an essay in June 2021 for the *Los Angeles Times* titled "You Shouldn't Need a College Degree to have a Decent Life in America." It was part of a project by the editorial board about how we might rethink the way we live after the pandemic. I wrote, "Not everyone, regardless of race or socioeconomics, wants or should need a four-year college degree. Education inflation not only leaves graduates (and even more, college dropouts) with crippling debt loads, but contributes to inequality and hampers the ability of many a bright student to enter the middle class."[4]

I didn't realize it at the time, but in many ways that column would prove prophetic. The pandemic, with the subsequent great resignation and labor shortage, spurred more employers into looking at applicants' skills rather than what level of formal education they had reached. At the same time, the Black Lives Matter movement prompted employers to take a serious look at hiring more people of color, and since Black and Latino applicants were less likely to have a bachelor's degree, those employers needed to look for smarter ways to hire and train new employees. Remote classes made both employers and job seekers more aware of the possibilities in online education, including MOOCs (massive open online courses) that are often free.

Other mainstream media began taking note. An October 2021 piece in the *New York Times* was headlined "College Degrees Are Overrated."[5] A July 2021 op-ed in the *Washington Post* titled "The majority of Americans lack a college degree. Why do so many employers require one?" targeted "three seemingly innocuous words—'bachelor's degree required'" as the root of serious damage to workers and the economy. The author of the *Post* op-ed, Byron Auguste, CEO of the organization Opportunity@Work, which advocates for hiring people based on factors other than college degrees, added, "The damage falls hardest on Black, Latino and rural workers; screening for bachelor's degrees excludes nearly 80 percent of Latino workers, almost 70 percent of African Americans and more than 70 percent of rural Americans across all backgrounds.

"Unless a college education is relevant to the work, it should be illegal to require a degree, just as it's illegal to hire applicants by race or sex," Auguste wrote.[6]

Businesses hurt themselves, too, when they shut the door against anyone without a four-year degree, according to a 2017 Harvard Business School report titled "Dismissed by Degrees."

"Degree inflation hurts the average American's ability to enter and stay in the workforce," the report says. "Many middle-skills jobs synonymous with middle-class lifestyles and upward mobility—such as supervisors, support specialists, sales representatives, inspectors and testers, clerks, and secretaries and administrative assistants—are now considered hard-to-fill jobs because employers prefer candidates who are college graduates."[7]

Companies pay more for college graduates even though they often find that those without degrees have skills that are just as good, the Harvard report said. "Employers that sought a graduate supervisor of office workers offered a mean real-time salary of $65,200 per year. Employers that did not insist on a college degree paid supervisors of office workers a mean real-time salary of $51,100 per year." And yet, the report said that "employers perceive the performance of non-degree workers to be remarkably close to that of college graduates in the same job." The workers without degrees required no more oversight in their jobs and were promoted just as quickly as the graduates.

College grads leave those jobs faster, seeking greener fields. Turnover is bad for business; it takes time and money to recruit, hire, and train someone new. Institutional memory is valuable. Employers are starting to recognize this.

But even as the job world produces more opportunities, you can't just emerge from high school and expect hot job prospects to fall into your lap. (You also can't expect that simply by emerging from college with a bachelor's degree. I know one young man who majored in environment and did a year in AmeriCorps, but then he couldn't find a job in his field because he hadn't given enough thought to gaining practical experience. It's unclear why he didn't go into the Environmental Conservation Corps, a branch of AmeriCorps that would have given him relevant skills and contacts. As a result, the best job he could get afterward was as a retail clerk in a sporting-goods store.) You need to know what's possible, what's available, and how to go after it. It's tougher to search for a post–high school career than to search for a college to attend, yet high schools pay a lot less attention to this part of counseling.

Did you know that one of the fastest-growing fields is makeup artists for the entertainment industry, with average salaries for experienced people well into the six figures?

It's still largely left to you—students and recent high school grads—to figure out one of the biggest decisions of your lives. That's why this book exists, for the millions who don't feel ready for college right now—or ever. My hope is to awaken you, as well as your parents, school counselors, and future employers, to the realization that not having a degree isn't necessarily a liability or an embarrassment. It doesn't mean leading a second-class life. I hope that if you have doubts about whether college is for you, you will think about using the four years you would have spent at college in other ways, ways that might bring you a long way toward the kind of life you seek.

•

Let's talk about some history. How did we get here, anyway? It's been a long, convoluted path.

During the 1970s, '80s, and '90s, a college degree made an enormous difference in a student's earning power, according to Richard Vedder, an emeritus professor of economics at Ohio University. At the same time, college tuition was much cheaper.

In 1985, the average cost of a year at college was less than $6,000. By 2022, tuition and fees cost on average more than $38,000, and that's not counting room and board. If the cost of college rose only as much as general inflation over that time, the cost today would be about $16,550—less than half of what families are paying.

The reasons are complicated. One of them is that colleges charge so much because they can. Student loans are easily available, which make it possible for young people to attend college in the short term and keeps demand high. There are legitimate increases in costs—a college education isn't easily automated, and its staff are paid well because they are experts in their fields. But US colleges often are administration-heavy—the number of nonacademic administrators and professionals more than doubled in twenty-five years, according to a 2014 report by the New England Center for Investigative Reporting, far outpacing the growth in student or professor populations. There has also been, at some colleges, a sort of "academic arms race" in which institutions of higher education pay large amounts of money to draw star faculty and researchers.

Adding to degree inflation was the maturing of the first of the echo boomers—offspring of the baby boomers—in the 1990s. Their parents were more likely to be college-educated than previous generations and expected their children to accomplish even more academically and financially, which to them naturally meant having at least the same level of formal education. In addition, the 1980s were economic boom years. Families had the money for college without having to take out second mortgages. College was clearly a worthwhile investment for those who could afford it.

When Stephen Schneider began working as a school counselor at Sheboygan South High School in Wisconsin in the mid-1990s, US high schools were judged by how many of their students went to college—which is still largely true. "If that's the measure of success for the school, then I'm going to do everything to get kids into college," he said.

Counselors nationwide became gun-shy about even suggesting anything other than college to students, lest parents accuse them of trying to force their children into lesser futures. The college push at Sheboygan South made sense when 80 percent of its graduating seniors were saying they would head to four-year college right after graduation.

That was what they said in surveys, anyway. Then there was the reality.

In 2011, National Student Clearinghouse data became available that changed everything.

It turned out that only half of the students at Stephen's school were actually going to college, even though what they were hearing from their counselors was college, college, college.

Many were simply checking the default box of college, Stephen conjectures, or perhaps they were ashamed to say they had different plans—or worse, no plans.

"We had been underserving so many students," he said. "We'd been missing the mark for years."

Sheboygan South has been one of a relatively few schools to overhaul its guidance program to help the students who were being overlooked, which in an area like Sheboygan, with its strong manufacturing-industry base, generally means helping students find their way into well-paid jobs in the skilled trades. Unfortunately, it doesn't help guide them to the many other possible careers without a college degree.

The advantage of a college education has been shrinking since the start of this century, Richard Vedder said, in part because of the overabundance of graduates. They were able to find jobs, but a hefty percentage of them were hired only for the jobs that previously hadn't required a college degree. They became office managers, aides, and salespeople—jobs that required organization, social skills, and smarts but that *didn't* need four years of college education.

In fact, according to the Department of Labor, as many as 17 *million* college graduates in 2020 were working in jobs that didn't require a college degree at the time. More than a third of all college graduates were "underemployed" in 2019—meaning working in jobs that didn't require a college degree. The number was even higher for recent graduates.

Why do employers hire overqualified people? For many, hiring college grads became a loose proxy for "smarts" or the willingness to work hard at something (a college degree) for years. It was the lazy boss's way of determining whether an applicant had the discipline and basic reading, writing, math, and critical-thinking skills to do the job. To be fair, high schools were pumping out too many students who lacked these basic skills. Unfortunately, this meant that many a bright high school grad with great skills was automatically ruled out.

But after the turn of the century, many employers were less enamored with college grads. The majority of employers in 2013 thought that half or fewer college grads had what it took to be promoted, according to Britannica ProCon.org. And close to a third of college grads felt their higher education hadn't prepared them well for the work world.[8]

Some of the sheen was coming off college education, but it got a boost during the Obama administration. Microsoft cofounder Bill Gates—himself a college dropout—became very involved in education issues and made increasing the number of college graduates a major campaign. He raised the specter of Americans not being prepared for twenty-first-century jobs. It was a refrain that was picked up by the Obama administration, but for good reason.

It's not that the country doesn't have enough college graduates. The problem is that college education isn't distributed equitably. Low-income Black and Latino students have been much less likely to attend college. That needed to change in order to uplift populations that otherwise would be stuck in low-paying jobs and to give bright, hardworking young people an equal opportunity to show what they could do.

Unfortunately, the "college for all" movement became overhyped. If high schools had previously been under pressure to send students to college, they now faced serious heat because of it. There's been some progress in the number of Black students attending college as a result, but also some fallback. And that's led to organizations such as Opportunity@ Work, whose philosophy is that low-income Black and Latino teenagers are at a particularly unfair disadvantage from the "college for all" movement because if they're *not* attending college—and most of them aren't—no one is creating a way for them to develop their talents and join the middle class.

"If you look at our country today and you look at all the jobs that pay $60,000 or more, on paper 79 percent of them require you to have a four-year degree just to compete for the job," Maurice Jones, director of OneTen, said during a recent federal webinar. "And yet . . . 66 percent of the workforce ages 25 and above do not have a four-year degree." That number is higher for the Black workforce: 76 percent.

The mission of OneTen is to encourage the hiring and advancement of one million Black people who lack a four-year degree, using a "skills-first" approach.

Four-year college graduates still, on average, make more money than those with two-year degrees—$19,000. And they average about $30,000 to $36,000 more than those with a high school diploma. But that doesn't take into account the cost of college, the annual weight of college loans, or the lack of earning during college years. And remember that the diploma group includes people who get no training or meaningful experiences beyond high school and go on to minimum-wage jobs. That's not where you're headed. In addition, better-paying options are opening up for high school grads. You'll learn about those and how to enter those fields in coming chapters.

Meanwhile, the Georgetown study on earnings by college grads and those with an associate's degree found that what matters more than the degree is the field of study. While liberal-arts majors often struggle after graduation, tech- and science-oriented jobs pay better and offer a more secure career, with or without a college degree. But it's worth noting that technical and engineering opportunities can be volatile, with waves of hiring and layoffs.

•

There's a lot of talk about how the United States should have tuition-free college, just as Germany and some other European nations do. But that movement ignores a lot of realities about higher education in Germany.

The German government can afford tuition-free college partly because relatively few students are accepted to college in the first place—about 24 percent of German high school students go on to university, compared with about 44 percent of American high school students, according to Research.com.[9] And college in Germany is not the fun-filled social and athletic center that describes most four-year schools in this country. Most German students live at home or rent a room with a family and commute to school. Dormitories are few. Class sizes are very large. There isn't much time spent with professors or advisers. Students are expected to be fully responsible for themselves and keep up with their work independently. Often, their grades come solely from a final exam, or perhaps a midterm as well. Team sports are a much smaller part of the scene—when they exist at all. The schools generally don't offer much in the way of extracurricular activities, though many students engage in these through clubs they organize on their own. Free university does not include room and board, so significant numbers of students end up in debt paying for that. Professors complain that their schools aren't able to do the same levels of research as US universities do and that the schools are overcrowded and stretched thin.

Germans are less intent on university as the only path to success because the country has long had a separate vocational track in which high school students can move into well-paid, respected jobs.

•

I particularly like this quote from Opportunity@Work: "We celebrate the dignity of all work and the dignity of every working person, especially those with overlooked skills." It reminds me of the attitude my father taught me: What people did for a living didn't matter. Whether they did it right, with care and concern for the quality of their work, was what gave their jobs value.

Our regard for plumbers is low—until the toilet is backed up and we have houseguests. Why don't we, as Germany does, make sure that our skilled workers in all fields receive both a family-supporting wage and the respect of our society?

A college degree in this country certainly has many valuable aspects. We wouldn't want brain surgeons or freeway architects to be people without extensive formal education. I'm not a fan of those who denigrate colleges and seek to weaken them; every society needs its great thinkers and researchers. But a bachelor's degree is not necessary in order to succeed financially, have an interesting and fulfilling career, contribute to the world, or even be a well-educated person and great thinker.

This book is a call to action to erase the confusion between having a degree and having the smarts and skills needed to succeed. It's a blueprint for the myriad avenues of learning and fulfillment open to those who don't want, can't afford, or aren't ready for the college pathway.

So far, I've been focusing mostly on the financials of alternative pathways to your future. Everyone has to consider how to make their way financially in the world. But there's a lot more to a thriving life than how much money you earn. What you'll learn about in this book are opportunities to support yourself through volunteering—yes, you read that right—as well as by creating. You'll find inspiring examples of people who started their own successful businesses without a four-year degree, including one who used her yacht to support her family. You'll also read about some of the unusual careers the military offers—dog handler, anyone?—and options abroad, outdoors, and through short-term training programs. The list is seemingly endless, and the internet has opened up entirely new possibilities. Opportunities abound to find jobs, reach audiences, and promote your skills and products. The world of apprenticeship—learning about a career as a paid trainee—shrank in the US for decades but now is making a comeback as a path to a rewarding career, according to the US Department of Labor. More employers are realizing that requiring degrees for many jobs is foolish.

My hope is that if a college path is not right for you, this book will help guide you to find the future that fits. When I was discussing this book with my newspaper colleagues over lunch one day, one of them expressed concern that loosening the pressure to attend college would mean lowering our expectations for what students can achieve. My reply was: "Why shouldn't a good life without four years of college be just as great an achievement?"

•

Antonio Santos wakes up happy every morning, because it's another day he'll be doing what he loves: editing videos. It doesn't hurt that at age twenty-eight, Tony, as he likes to be called, is making more than $100,000 a year doing it.

At least the income will help him pay off the $70,000 in remaining student debt from colleges he never finished because he found they weren't giving him the kind of education he craved. His skills are largely self-taught.

Tony's story is a perfect illustration of what it often takes to thrive without a four-year degree and why college is not the right path for everyone. Growing up in a suburb of Chicago, he knew early on what gave him great pleasure; he'd been editing videos as a hobby starting at age fifteen. But, like many students, he assumed he couldn't make a living doing what he loved, so he entered college not knowing what he really wanted. Studying science and engineering seemed like a smart way to make a living. But it wasn't interesting to him, so he left after a year. He then went to another college, this time in his chosen field of the arts. He found the instruction rigid and unhelpful and left again after a year. "I felt like my teachers kept stifling any creative ideas I had," he said.

Like many of the more than 30 percent of students who don't complete their college educations, he was buried in debt with no degree to show for it.

Through friends, he learned about openings in video editing and built up his skills and experience. These jobs didn't pay well and weren't regular for the most part, but he was building a résumé and developing skills to show off, including editing for a YouTube channel.

And then a friend from college told him that Thomas Frank, a popular YouTuber known for his educational videos on how to handle many aspects of life, was looking for an editor. Tony looked at the opening and felt unqualified; he had no experience with the editing system Frank used. But he applied anyway, asking Frank to give him one month to learn everything he needed to know. Frank was impressed by his willingness to learn and his familiarity with the deadline and other demands of producing YouTube videos.

"He taught me with a fire hose," Tony said. "It was nonstop information. But that was what turned my life around."

He moved to Denver, where Frank was located. For the first time, he was working for a man who was committed to the quality of the videos being produced and willing to pay to keep that quality high.

He also got a lot of his editing education for free on YouTube and other sites. "I legit learned 99 percent of everything I know online. Even though I went to art school for a year, nothing that I learned there has compared to the internet." Now he's paying it forward with his own YouTube channel full of videos teaching editing skills. The conclusion to this book will inform you about these and other nontraditional ways of learning that are free or low-cost.

In Tony's case, success came from networking, finding a mentor, and working his way up from the bottom with low-paying jobs that taught skills. That plus the chutzpah to apply for a job for which he wasn't quite qualified brought him the success and happiness he'd dreamed of finding.

Tony was lucky in other ways. His parents had always supported whatever path he chose, telling him that as long as he was a good person and found a way to contribute to the world, they were happy. Even so, it took a lot of commitment and belief in what he might be able to achieve. In 2018, when he made less than $1,000 the entire year, his sister helped him out financially. But he had to endure the perception that his efforts were lagging. An acquaintance of his was considering going to trade school to learn how to be a medical assistant even though he wasn't excited about the job. Someone else told that acquaintance to go for it or he'd "end up like Tony." That hurt.

The result? After two years of expensive trade-school education, this acquaintance found he really wasn't happy in the small confines of a doctor's office, doing repetitive tasks. He became a specialized truck driver with no particular educational requirements, making more money and enjoying being out and about.

Meanwhile, ending up like Tony is looking pretty good. He's a big advocate for starting out by following your dream, no matter how impossible it sounds. Sometimes that means college, other times not.

For a long time, editors in the film industry were trained through apprenticeships. Then, for the most part, having a bachelor's degree was the norm, and a specialized master's degree in filmmaking has become more common. But things might be turning around. A friend of Tony's works at one of the big film companies. Its work includes animated films, Tony's special love. He asked his friend how a person like himself, without a college degree, could possibly get a job there. All the company's listings in his field say a bachelor's degree is required.

His friend said that, in truth, the human resources staff no longer bases its hires on that particular requirement. Meanwhile, a bachelor's degree continues to be listed as a prerequisite for all its jobs. Imagine how many talented people that company will miss out on hiring until it changes its listings to match the reality. And the film editor's union has brought back its apprenticeship program—with no bachelor's degree required.

COLLEGE OR NOT?

It's not a matter of whether four-year college is "better" than forging your own path for now. It's a great opportunity for some people and the wrong fit for others. Both sets of people should have the same shot at a fulfilling, financially stable life. The internet has made it easier for non–college graduates to find other paths to their life dreams, and more employers are finding that people without bachelor's degrees.

THE PROS OF A BACHELOR'S DEGREE	THE PROS OF UNCOLLEGING
Looked on favorably by employers	Saving a whole lot of money
A network of colleagues and possibly alumni	Meeting a wider variety of people
Learning new knowledge and ways of thinking	Deciding what you want to learn instead
Exploring your life interests via study	Exploring your life interests via doing

The fun of campus life	The fun of exploring far beyond a college campus's boundaries
On average, college grads earn more	Getting a head start on your career and life
Some professions truly need people to have advanced formal education	More employers are hiring people who don't have degrees for good jobs
You've always liked school and love to read	You've always hated school and read only when necessary
"If I get it done now, I'll be set up for life."	"I can always choose college, when I know better what I want from it, have saved money, and might get tuition help from my employer."

The opportunities for people without a bachelor's degree are better now than they've been for decades and will get better in coming years. It's too bad that the United States has, for far too long, ignored the many talented people who aren't headed for four-year college, while European countries have actively created, promoted, and funded multiple pathways to success. Here are some of the common-sense policy changes that need to be made by governments, schools, and employers to fix this:

- State and local governments need to jump on the movement by adopting policies that eliminate college degrees as a requirement for public jobs unless there's a specific reason for that. Former President Donald Trump got the ball rolling on that by signing an executive order that did this very thing for federal jobs. At least eight states followed with very similar policies; by the time you read this, it's probably more. Now it's time to make this the standard in government jobs.

- School counselors need to be trained better on the many alternatives to college and required to talk to students about these options, giving them information on how to get started, in addition to the two alternatives—the trades and the military—that students hear about now.

- The federal and state departments of education must take the initiative in pushing for more white-collar apprenticeship opportunities to build a system more like the one in Switzerland, so that young people can enter such well-paid fields as being a bank executive without a four-year degree. Employers need to step up to provide these paid apprenticeships, which will help them find and keep well-trained staff.

- High schools are already starting to return to the days where "shop class" is a valid option for students. The country is expected to have a shortage of 400,000 welders by 2024, the American Welding Society estimated. But beyond typical shop, more schools are needed that provide training that sends students straight into white-collar jobs. Intensive "coding camp" programs would help students who now pay about $10,000 for such training. The Los Angeles high school that actor George Clooney worked to get started prepares students for jobs in the film and television industries, which have all but required college degrees.

- Employers, both profit and nonprofit, should reexamine their outdated rules requiring bachelor's degrees for jobs that don't really need degrees, developing a "skills before degrees" approach. Many of these jobs didn't require a college education decades ago and haven't changed much since then even though the education requirements have. These businesses are hurting themselves as well as the next generation of employees with a requirement that often has no common sense behind it.

- Colleges need to rethink themselves. That doesn't mean the traditional four years on campus, with sports teams and parties and extracurriculars, needs to disappear. But colleges will have to get more serious about reducing expenses in various ways. Shrinking administration and the number of sports teams is just a start. They could offer different levels of attainment, just as community colleges do now, including certificates and associate's degrees, and in chapter 12, you'll learn about a school that does. They could allow associate's degrees for students who initially seek a bachelor's degree but then decide a four-year degree isn't for them, so that they haven't spent all that time and money for education with nothing to show for it. They could consider switching to a system like the one in England, where many majors require only three years to graduation. Working with employers, they could set up apprenticeship programs. It would help to give credit toward graduation for relevant work experience and life accomplishments and make learning more experiential. The Evergreen State College, which you'll read about in chapter 12, has been at the forefront of changing the college experience. More schools should follow its example.

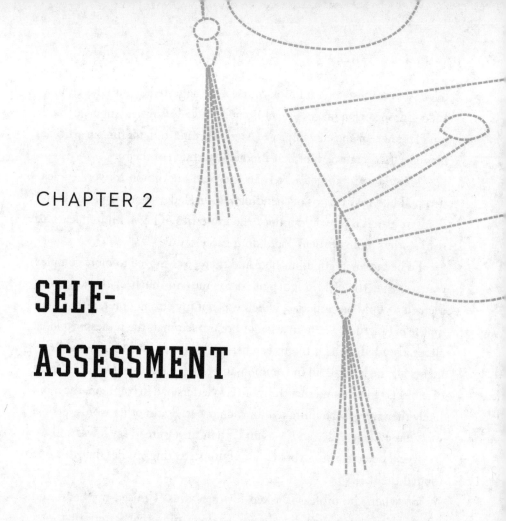

CHAPTER 2

SELF-ASSESSMENT

How did I happen to become a journalist? I grew up in a family that read multiple newspapers daily, but that didn't lead me to consider it as an occupation at the time. I wasn't on my high school paper. Journalism wasn't what I studied in college. In fact, my college didn't even offer courses in journalism; in that liberal arts school, journalism was considered a trade, not an academic pursuit.

It took a sudden epiphany and then a hardheaded and unsparing assessment of my likes, strengths—and yes, weaknesses—to decide to enter the field where I would end up working for more than forty-five years.

My major was linguistics, and I loved studying the nature of language: the sounds, the history, the philosophy, and the psychology of it. In addition to classes on those topics, I took courses, as suggested by my adviser, in an Indo-European language (French), a non–Indo-European language (modern Hebrew), an ancient language (Anglo-Saxon), and, for fun, an artificial language (Esperanto). Not that I remember much of them.

The plan was to get a PhD in the field and go on to work in academia. I had rosy visions of spending laid-back days pondering ideas and doing research that would unlock the mysteries of how children learn to read so that more of them could do it successfully.

I'd been picking up hints here and there, as I moved to more complex courses, that the field might not be for me. So much of the key work seemed focused on minutiae, which was not my strong point, rather than on the big picture. Then, in a senior honors seminar, the professor told us about a study in which the researchers figured out how many visual elements all the letters had in common and flashed letters superfast in front of subjects. They found that the more two letters had in common, the more likely they were to be mistaken for each other. So, in other words, people were more likely to say an F was an E than they were to say it was a G.

We'd been learning about a lot of uninteresting studies, but this one topped them all.

So when the professor asked for questions, I raised my hand and asked, "You mean they did a study to determine that letters that look more alike really do look more alike?" She acknowledged that it seemed a little silly but said that this was where the field of linguistics was at the time, and these were the kinds of questions that had to be nailed down by academics. This was the field I'd studied so hard to enter.

Drilling down into tiny details that seemed obvious would frustrate someone like me no end. I needed to come up with a new career plan and fast.

That was when I sat down and took stock of myself.

I had always loved writing and been complimented by teachers and professors for doing it well. So, could I be a novelist? There would be no income for a long time, if ever, and my parents had done enough, supporting me through college. I had student loans to pay—though minor compared with what college grads face these days. Besides, I had no ideas for a novel!

My analytical skills were pretty good, so what about law? It would pay really well, but I felt I would be bored at work, from what I knew of the profession and the people in it. Besides, I hated having to dress up in office attire.

I even counted up the hours people generally spend at work and getting ready for work, versus hours spent in leisure-time activities. It turns out that people spend far more hours at work than they do at play, so it made sense to me to settle on a career that was fun, as opposed to unfun but more profitable. I was also mission-driven; I wanted my work to do good in the world.

Even more, I loved learning about pretty much everything. And yet, embarrassing as it was to admit, I was an intellectual dilettante. Just like with linguistics, I loved learning up to a certain point, but once things got into the weeds, I was easily bored.

One other little quirk: I did my best work on tight deadlines. I almost always wrote my papers the night before they were due. No outlines. No drafts. I would spread my research materials around and peck out a first and final draft on my Smith Corona portable typewriter.

It all added up to . . . journalism: Learn about everything—but not too much about anything. Experience new things and have an exciting workday. Report stories that could change lives. I could write for a living, and usually on tight deadline, straight from notes. I wouldn't get rich, but I'd get by financially.

Self-assessment was a cold and calculated way to decide my future. It also worked.

•

Michael B. Horn has made a career of studying the future of education, including why people go to college, when in their lives they do it, how it works out for them—and how it should change. Michael, who cowrote a book titled *Choosing College: How to Make Better Learning Decisions Throughout Your Life*, agrees with me that college is terrific for people who strongly prefer to go and know what they plan to get out of it and how. It works best for people who already like what college entails: study, lectures, thinking, and intense mental work. If you hated it in high school, you're probably going to hate it in college, where it's tougher and your chances of not making it are higher.

What are the worst reasons to go to college? According to Michael, it's when you can't think of anything else you would do or, even worse, when others—usually parents or school counselors—pressure you to go even though you're not excited about the idea. Among those who go for those reasons, a whopping 59 percent later say college was a big waste of money.

And yet, he said, school counselors don't seem to know much else they can tell students. In 1980, about a third of students were urged by their high schools to attend college. Some ten years later, when the "college for all" movement was taking off in the United States, it was twice that many.

Michael says—and I've noticed this myself—that school counselors tend to offer students three concrete options: college, skilled labor, or the military. There's nothing wrong with any of those choices. They're exactly right for some people. Joining a skilled labor force or signing up with the military can lead to some very surprising, lucrative, and fulfilling careers (see chapters 9 and 11). But the possibilities extend far beyond those. The truth is, school counselors are extremely busy people, usually responsible for advising too many students. They have been trained to think in terms of college readiness and might not be conversant in the changing dynamics of the workplace.

A community college in the Milwaukee, Wisconsin, area offers a gap year program that at least helps point the way to careers that students might find of interest. The ten-week intensive program pays students from families making less than $75,000 a year and exposes them to a wide variety of careers, visiting workplaces and meeting with employers and college officials. That would be a great program to expand nationwide for the many high school grads who aren't sure what their next step should be.

In the absence of those real-life experiences, this chapter provides four quizzes to help you decide what sorts of things might interest you for your future. The first will give you some guidance on whether college looks like the best choice for you *right now*. It might be, but even if it's not, that doesn't mean it never will be. You might work in a field and decide on a specific job that requires a bachelor's degree. You might start out with short-term training and then work up to better-paying jobs that call for a two-year associate's degree—and find that your work experience and maturity have made college work both easier for you and more attractive. You'll meet several people in this book who have done just that.

Another quiz will help you figure out whether you are likely to be successful in a career that doesn't require a degree. People who fall into this category tend to have a talent for networking and finding mentors to help guide them. They also aren't concerned about being judged for not getting a bachelor's degree.

The other two quizzes are more like the informal self-assessment process I put myself through when I switched to journalism. The three last quizzes combined will help you think more deeply about who you are and what you like doing and determine your own work style. Use your answers to go online and find career niches that suit your strengths, your likes, and your weak spots as well.

The best starting point for online career searching may well be AI platforms, which obtain information from a variety of solid sources and gather various kinds of data in one purposeful presentation (such as: Which jobs are good for disorganized film lovers who hate stress? Which are best for mission-driven idealists who love to create new computer programs?). For fun, I wondered whether there were good careers for intellectual dilettantes. It turns out there are. The first one listed by the platform was writer. So there you go.

That's just the first step, though. You can't rely on an AI platform or a search engine to determine your future. Once you've narrowed your list of possible careers or fields, there are three key additional steps. They take a little bit of work and initiative, but you will be that much further ahead of the pack when you do them.

In the fourth quiz, you will be asked to think about the things you like doing and that you actually do. There's little point in dreaming of being a nurse or doctor of phlebotomist if you are squeamish about physical things including blood. You can't be much of a teacher if the high-pitched sound of kids' voices drives you crazy. Think about careers as professionalized extensions of what you already love to do. Chances are, these also will be activities for which you have built some skill. As Michael Horn puts it, think in terms of work that gets your sense of energy going. At the same time, it's not enough to simply "follow your bliss." Is the work of developing competence in this vocation appealing to you?

Once you've settled on a few ideas, do some informational interviews. Contact someone who does that job and tell them you're interested in pursuing the same career and would be thankful for a half hour of their time to find out about the work they do. Chances are they'll give you as much time as you want once you get started. People love to talk about their jobs and get satisfaction out of feeling they're setting up the next generation for success. Or they might warn you about a long list of downsides that you had no idea existed.

If it's workable for you and them, doing the interview at their workplace would be ideal. That way, you're likely to get a tour as well as a better connection to your interviewee.

It's crucial to write down questions in advance and have plenty of them. Michael Horn suggests making them as specific as you can: *How do you start your workday? How much time do you spend in meetings? What kind of contact do you have with people during your work?* Do enough research on the job to have knowledgeable questions; people will regard you more highly and give you better information if you show you cared enough to do due diligence before you arrive.

This one is a little tougher: see if you can shadow someone who does the job you're interested in for at least a couple of days. Perhaps in schools of the future, there will be designated days in the academic calendar for this, and schools will have contacts to help set this up. But in all likelihood, that's not the reality for you. Plan on devoting some vacation days to shadowing and arrange things well in advance—it might involve navigating a bureaucracy (an education all by itself). Your informational interviewee may be able to set something up. Or try contacting a company's human resources department and see if they can possibly accommodate you. You can try looking into summer internships, but most formal internships are reserved for college students. Still, if your interest impresses the people you contact, they might just create an internship for you.

Most people, when considering college, visit the campuses that interest them. They ask alumni or current students about their experience. Many colleges hold weekends where accepted students can visit, sleeping in dorm rooms and talking to students, to see what college life is like. Why would you do anything less when considering a career?

•

Mei Pang's parents wanted her to become a certified public accountant —a practical, stable career that requires a bachelor's degree. She flunked physics twice, though, making her wonder about a future in a university setting. Even then, she tried the "what people tell me I should do" route by attending college, which didn't work out for her. She eventually found her niche as a social media influencer, but she would have found it much earlier had she learned to examine how she actually liked spending her time.

It's one of the newest jobs around, social media influencer. Influencers make real money from posting content on various social media sites, a phenomenon that began in the early 2010s. The trick, at first, is attracting followers, which is done in all kinds of ways. One influencer started with reviews of octopus dishes in local restaurants and then moved on to short, deadpan skits with his friends. Another educates the public about her indigenous background as she demonstrates jingle dances and sings songs that are a mix of Western and traditional. A third has made millions telling true stories of gruesome murders while applying her makeup. The money comes mostly from sponsors who pay the influencers to promote the companies' products—or send them swag to do the same. And for the successful ones, the money is big, though potentially short-lived.

Mei's niche is avant-garde makeup—slicking back her eyebrows with glue sticks and drawing lines on her face with dental floss. Sometimes, she'll mix things up by talking to strangers about her many tattoos, her sobriety, or her cat.

In her late twenties, Mei brings in a six-figure income, largely from sponsorships. With her 2.8 million TikTok followers amping up her fame, she scored a spot on the Savage X Fenty runway and forged brand collaborations with Urban Decay and NYX cosmetics.

"People basically know me for putting household items against my face to create a pattern."

Mei grew up outside Toronto, Canada. Her early encounters with Tumblr set her on a course for the arts. "It clicked for me," she recalled. "It set my soul on fire, and it's something that I could definitely do for the rest of my life."

Mei devoured creative content online. She was active on social media, posting in large part about her partying. And then she went to college.

Acceptance to OCAD, Canada's premier art university, felt like a win at first. For three years, Mei soldiered through OCAD's demanding curriculum, churning out six paintings a week and enduring regular critiques from faculty whose assessments felt arbitrary and wore her down into "a shell of who I was." With one year left to finish, she dropped out.

Mei then worked three jobs to cover her rent. She stocked the counters at a makeup retailer part-time and completed a cosmetic certification course. Eventually she landed a corporate gig as a receptionist at Inkbox, a temporary tattoo company. Two years later, the pandemic struck and erased her job.

Then she tried doing what she had felt drawn to from the start: social media, along with art and makeup. She used all that isolated pandemic time to build a presence on Instagram and YouTube. She got sober and started posting regularly, with intention and professionalism.

Brands started reaching out to her. By this time, she had a manager, who persuaded her to give TikTok a try despite her hesitancy. "The demographic was so young, right? And I was genuinely afraid to get cyberbullied by, like, twelve-year-olds."

Instead, she quickly amassed a following on the platform. Makeup tutorials dominate Mei's feed, but she also documents her life, which, as an influencer, appears stereotypically glamorous—Coachella one week, acroyoga in Costa Rica the next. What followers don't always see on-screen is Mei's discipline and unyielding focus: "I always feel the need to be doing something in order to be productive."

When she's not traveling, Mei has a routine. She wakes at 5:30 a.m., works on her online presence until about 10, practices yoga for an hour and a half, then tends to administrative tasks, wrapping up her workday at 3 p.m. When she travels, she still works. Yes, she was at Coachella, but she kept up with business from the mosh pit.

•

A three-hour talk with Wylie Stateman, the sound man for dozens of major movies, has me thinking more about sound than I have in my entire life.

Wylie has worked as sound editor or sound designer with directors such as Oliver Stone (*Wall Street, Alexander, Nixon*), Quentin Tarantino (*Kill Bill Vol. 1, Django Unchained, Inglourious Basterds*), and Wolfgang Peterson (*Air Force One, Troy, The Perfect Storm*). Now in his sixties, he has racked up nine Academy Award nominations and six BAFTA nominations, with one win. And the projects go on.

With a partner, he also owned a sound business that sold more than twenty years ago for $90 million. They distributed most of that money —$50 million—to their seventy most significant employees. Of the twelve or so who were made instant millionaires, Wylie said, more than half did not have a bachelor's degree—like Wylie himself.

Wylie is obviously an extreme talent at multiple activities, including entrepreneurialism and creativity. He also has an aptitude for and fascination with mechanical devices, which made him an earlier adopter of technology to create sound. But above all, he appears to have an innate ability to assess his strengths and weaknesses, which activities bring him joy and which ones bore him. That sense of self is what led him to avoid college, a decision that frustrated his college-educated parents.

It's not that Wylie has anything against higher education. His own kids have gone beyond a bachelor's degree to graduate school. But he has dyslexia, which made reading a slow frustration—and school and college work are heavily dependent on reading.

"I was a pretty mediocre student," he said. "So I became a good listener. I loved navigating the world through my ears."

So much so that his favorite album as a kid wasn't by any of the pop musicians of the time. It was an LP his father gave him of sounds: rockets, birds, trains, all kinds of sounds.

Wylie's grandfather would communicate with his family via reel-to-reel tape recordings, catching them up on what had been happening in his life. And Wylie would correspond back with recordings but add sounds to his monologues.

Another thing Wylie knew about himself: he craved being around creative people who were brimming with original ideas. A university didn't seem like the place where that would happen. Hollywood did. And it needed people who understood sound.

"The single piece of advice I give students that they've never heard from any of their teachers: Hollywood is a place where you don't need to start at the bottom and work your way up," Wylie said. "You can start where you want to be and work your way out."

In other words, start at a place that will let you do what you're aiming for, or as close to it as possible, and from that build a reputation that allows you to expand.

Case in point: After arriving in Hollywood, he trained as a movie projectionist but then learned that Sunn Classic Pictures in Park City, Utah, was recruiting. The production company was known for family fare such as *The Life and Times of Grizzly Adams*. They were willing to take beginners because they paid minimum wage—about $2 an hour, Wylie said. Since he was happy to work endless hours, he made enough to live.

What got him in the door as a sound man were his mechanical skills, including his projectionist know-how. Sunn desperately needed people who could run their machinery—and if Wylie could do that, he was told, they would start him as a sound editor.

During that time, Wylie was one of twenty Sunn employees mentored by a film school professor who had been brought on to set up the company's postproduction operations. That was where Wylie gained not just his first real training in sound but also an approach to problem-solving that involved rethinking things from various angles. That outside-the-box way of thinking would shape a lot of Wylie's approach to sound editing.

As he puts it, he looks at things "as if we fell from outer space and took an entirely new look at this."

But Park City wasn't Wylie's happy place, so he headed west again. Back in Hollywood, he was offered a job doing sound editing at one of the many sound studios that dotted the area in the 1970s. But on the way back to his car, Wylie happened to pass another sound studio and dropped in. It turned out that the studio was "in crisis," he said, over its most recent project, which happened to be the now-classic movie *Coal Miner's Daughter*.

The supervising sound editor assigned him a train scene and said, "Let's see what you can do with this." Wylie didn't want to work from canned audio of trains. "I designed a really beautiful train sound," he said, a softer sound than most train scenes, with some plaintive notes in it. He spent the next few months as an uncredited sound designer on the film, and from then on he worked only on mainstream projects.

Wylie is known in the industry for his belief that sound isn't just a part of postproduction. It has to be a part of the thinking and creation process during production, which allows him to develop novel ideas. So he won't accept a project unless he first gets to read the script, even though his dyslexia—plus copious note-taking—makes the read a fourteen-hour process.

The company Wylie sold, Soundelux, produced more than film sound. It also created about one hundred audiobooks, the sound effects for Universal Studios theme parks, and many projects that involved sound.

Wylie doesn't just work in sound. He also *thinks* about it, ponders its complexity. What's the difference between music and sound, and does such a difference even exist? Why are some sounds beautiful to people, some calming, and others grating? The temporal nature of sound fascinates him too. Freeze a frame from a film and you still have a picture, he notes—but you no longer have the sound. Sound, like movement, happens only in the moment. I haven't stopped noticing sounds since we talked.

QUIZ

Here's a quiz to help clarify whether a four-year college is the right choice for you immediately after high school. There are no right or wrong answers; the quiz is aimed at getting you to do some deeper thinking about your options and which ones sound right to you at this point in your life:

1. How much do you know about what you want to do for a living?
    a. I know exactly the career I want, and it requires a college degree.
    b. Though I know the career I want, that could change. I'd be interested in a way of trying it out before I start college.

c. I generally know the field I'm interested in entering, but not the specifics of exactly what I want to do.

d. I don't know what I want to do with my life. I'm hoping college will give me some idea.

2. How well prepared are you financially for a four-year college?

a. I'm set financially. My family can afford the schools I'm interested in attending and where I'm likely to be admitted.

b. I've looked into the costs, and my family can afford part of it. I'm not really sure how I'd pay for the rest.

c. I've looked into the costs and can afford part of it, but I'd need to take out some serious student loans. However, the profession I'll be entering will clearly allow me to pay off those loans in less than a decade.

d. I've looked into the costs, and it would be really hard to come up with the money without getting into serious debt. I don't know what I'll be doing for a living, so I'm a little scared about paying off the debt.

3. How well have you researched the education and other training required to get started in your chosen profession?

a. I have looked into this carefully, and there's no way to enter this field without a college degree.

b. I've looked into it, and most of the people who do this work seem to have college degrees, but I'm not sure it's required.

c. I don't really know what kind of education I need, but a college degree has got to help, right?

d. I don't know what I want to do. But my school counselor said I should go to college and all my friends are doing it.

4. What are your financial and personal plans?

a. Being prosperous right away in a highly respected profession is very important to me.

b. I want to make a lot of money, but I don't need to be in a profession to do that.

c. I want to make a good living, but it's also important to me to know I'm pursuing work that will feel interesting and fulfilling, maybe even fun.

d. I want to try the adventures life offers; I don't need to be rich or be some kind of VIP for that to happen.

5. What's your learning style?

a. I've done well in high school and enjoy good lectures and challenging assignments.

b. I don't like teachers deciding what I need to know. I can study on my own and learn the things that interest me.

c. I have my own style of doing things that often goes against the grain, but it usually works for me.

d. I learn better by doing things and practicing them in real life.

6. What are the reasons that most interest you in a four-year college education?

a. I love learning from knowledgeable, intelligent people. I want to learn deeper ways to think and broaden my areas of study.

b. I want to get a better-paying job.

c. Living in a dorm, making friends, going to games and parties, and just getting that full college experience are appealing to me. The classes I take are of less importance to me.

d. My parents are pretty determined that I should go.

7. How important is it to you to have at least a bachelor's degree?

a. I can't imagine not having a college degree. No one respects people who aren't highly educated.

b. I think a college degree will help me make more money, but if I could earn as much without a degree, that works for me!

c. I don't know how to go about applying for jobs or making a living without a college degree.

d. If someone shows me the way, I'd like to build up experience that makes me a smarter and more creative person without having a piece of paper.

8. How important is a social and professional network, and how do you go about getting one?

a. With its alumni office and connections, a college is the way for me to meet people who can help me.

b. I'm kind of an introvert and need structured groups to start meeting people.

c. A network isn't that important to me. I'm going to get ahead by just doing a great job at whatever I do.

d. A network is hugely important, and I'm building one all the time. I'm not afraid to reach out to people and ask them things, and in turn I try to help out people who ask me. Everyone I meet is a potential friend or contact.

9. What have your experiences been in the world of work outside school?

a. I've had outside jobs, and they gave me a good idea of the kind of work I want to do—which definitely requires a college degree and almost certainly grad school.

b. I haven't really had outside jobs because I study pretty hard and do a lot of extracurriculars to build a good résumé for college applications.

c. I've had some interesting jobs, and I learned something from every one of them.

d. I've had a bunch of outside jobs and have even had them lead to offers for full-time work. It's been tempting.

10. What would you be doing if all colleges were closed for the next four years and there was nowhere to go for a formal higher education?

    a. I would be reading a lot of books, finding tutors, and practicing my math skills to try to learn more academically on my own, so I'd be ahead when they reopen.

    b. I would get any job I could to save up money to attend for when they reopen.

    c. I would try out some jobs I've always thought might interest me to see if I actually like doing them, and then see after a few years whether I'm on my way or whether I should think about college. I'm kind of tired of sitting in classrooms and writing papers. I want some real-world experience at this point.

    d. I'd use my creative and interpersonal skills to start a business.

Scoring: For each A answer, add 1 point, a B is 2 points, C is 3, and D is 4. If your score adds up to 10 to 25, you probably will feel most comfortable in college during your years after high school. If your score is 26 to 30, it's worth examining your options outside a four-year school.

YOUR STYLE

If you pick a career that doesn't fit your work and personal style, chances are you either won't stay there for long or will feel fairly miserable and inadequate through most of your career. It's rarely worth spending your life that way, no matter how much money is involved. A good income should enhance and stabilize your life, not try to make up for core unhappiness.

This questionnaire doesn't have a scoring mechanism. Instead, it's meant to encourage you to get to know yourself in the most honest and authentic way so that, in concert with the other quizzes, you can find your most likely paths to a rewarding future, whether or not you choose college. Pick just one answer for each question; most of us can relate to multiple kinds of work, but think about what is most *you*, because you'll be spending a lot of hours doing that for years to come.

The quiz also asks you to think about your life from all aspects: financial, social, family, living, values, and environment. It's important to go through this process; too often, people see a job that looks cool or brings in lots of money or sounds exciting and set their sights on it without thinking about whether it makes any sense for their personalities and priorities.

My personal example is pretty simple: I love tight deadlines and do my best work on them. I've always enjoyed writing and do it well. Journalism came to mind immediately; I then checked it out against other aspects of my personality, interests, and talents.

1. Which of these is the most important to you when considering a job?
   a. Prosperity
   b. I need to make a decent living but don't need to be rich; financial stability in an interesting job would make me happy.
   c. Doing something good for people or the planet
   d. Getting to use and challenge my brain
   e. Good work-life balance so that I can spend time with family and on my outside interests
   f. Adventure and excitement

2. What kind of people contact do you crave in a job?
   a. I want to work remotely; I do best in quiet places and want to spend my spare time on my individual interests.
   b. I want to work in an office with skilled, interesting people who will inspire me to be my best self.
   c. I want to work with fun, creative people where there's lots of brainstorming and camaraderie.
   d. I want to work with customers; it's fun to get people on your side and excited about what you're doing.

  e. I want to work with the public, making a difference in the lives of people who need my help.

  f. I would like to deal with people as little as possible. Put me somewhere with nature or animals.

3. How would you most like to spend your work time?

  a. Leading others. I often see a smart way to get things done, and things would probably run better if I could show people the way.

  b. Analyzing problems and fixing them

  c. Talking to the people who aren't coworkers, whether they're students or members of the public or customers

  d. Bringing my creativity into my daily life to make the work more fulfilling and interesting

  e. Lots of downtime would be nice. I don't want to be a busy beaver all day.

  f. Working with my hands

4. What kind of workplace do you crave?

  a. Certain kinds of stress are fun. I want to be in a fast-paced workplace where people are excited and things are humming.

  b. Helping others is important. I want to work in an organization that's trying to do good in the world with coworkers who are as committed as I am.

  c. One with regular and not overly long hours. I don't want to be taken advantage of by my workplace; I'll work hard while I'm there but then I want to go enjoy my life.

  d. Nothing is as interesting as creative work and people. I want to be in a place where my creativity is appreciated and where other creative people will turn me on to new ways of doing things.

    e. I want to travel a lot.

    f. I want the kind of job that will let me switch to part-time over the course of my career. I'll have family obligations and other projects I want to pursue; a life of full-time work would feel like too much of a trap.

5. What kind of work do you want to do during the day?
    a. Something that requires out-of-the-box thinking.
    b. I'm really analytical and want to use that part of my brain to solve knotty problems.
    c. I've always liked the sciences. I can really get into the details.
    d. I've always been drawn to creative pursuits like making videos, drawing, writing, photography, or designing things.
    e. Work that's at least somewhat different from what I did the day before. I need variety in my life, learning totally new things, getting new experiences.
    f. I'm mission-driven. I want to make the world a better place.

6. What's your style of getting your work done?
    a. Multitasking is more fun and gives me the variety I crave.
    b. I love to burrow into a single task and not get distracted by a bunch of other demands.
    c. I'm better off with short-term tasks. I get lost with big, complicated projects.
    d. Need those deadlines. I'll procrastinate without them.
    e. I like to plan and organize my time and priorities for the day.
    f. I'm more comfortable with someone giving me direct instructions and a schedule so that I know exactly what to do and when to stay on track.

7. How tidy is your desk?
    a. Desk? I was supposed to use my desk? I mainly use that to throw random stuff on.
    b. It's a total mess of paper and other items, and sometimes I lose stuff there. Getting it straightened out takes so much time, and then it just gets messed up again in no time.
    c. It's a major mess, but I've got it organized in my brain so I can find anything I need in less than a minute.
    d. It's not military-neat, but it's not too bad. A little messy.
    e. It's very neat. I can think more clearly when it's organized.
    f. I keep my whole room tidy so that I can find things. I have a busy life and a lot to organize, and that works better if there's not a ton of clutter around.

8. How big a role does the latest tech play in your life?
    a. I use it when it's necessary, but it's not a big thing for me.
    b. I'm a little afraid of it, though of course I use it. It's going to take over our jobs. Pretty soon it will be writing our books, making our movies, and robotically unplugging the toilet. What will be left for us?
    c. I love the tools available to make my life easier.
    d. I'm fascinated by the ways it's developing, and though I have no interest in coding, I am interested in keeping on top of the latest developments.
    e. I want to be the person who creates the next big thing in tech.

9. How good are your communication skills?
    a. I'm not really a word person. Coming up with what I want to say can be a struggle.
    b. I communicate nonverbally, through my actions and my facial expressions.

c. I'm okay talking to people, but writing is another matter. I kind of freeze up.

d. I communicate easily in writing but tend to be a little stiffer talking to people when it really matters, like in interviews or talking to teachers.

e. I feel pretty comfortable talking with different kinds of people, and my English is good. Just don't make me do public speaking!

f. I'm articulate and find it easy to speak in ways that impress people.

How do you use all this? Let's say you're like me and you like to be revving at work, moving fast, with tremendous focus and concentration, and you're good at multitasking. Sure, daily journalism fits with that—but so does being an air traffic controller, a job that requires training but not a bachelor's degree. Even in the lowest-paid states, according to the Bureau of Labor Statistics, air traffic controllers earn about $80,000, and in the highest-paid states—which are not always the most expensive places to live—they earn more like $130,000.

If you like science, working with people, and doing good for the world, medicine and health care might be for you. Maybe you'd like to start as a nursing assistant, make money right away, and then build up your educational credits to be a registered nurse.

If you prefer to concentrate hard for long periods of time, prefer a quiet place to work—ideally at home alone—and are analytical, but your communication skills aren't that strong, programming would be one of your good fits. Highly organized, articulate, and good with people? Top-notch office managers make up to $200,000 a year.

Spend some time with these questions and your answers. Try writing down the answers you gave so they are all together; it's a summation of your work style. Think about the person who emerges from these answers, and then use them and the subsequent quizzes as a base for searching out the kinds of fields that might suit you best.

LIFE WITHOUT A DEGREE: ARE YOU READY?

After interviewing dozens of people who have built meaningful lives without a high school diploma, as well as the people who help them, coach them, and act as mentors, I've noticed that these young adults tend to have several traits in common. Here's a questionnaire to get an idea of how many of those traits you appear to have.

1. How do you react when multiple people are telling you you're making a mistake but you feel certain you're on the right course?
   a. It's important to listen to people who have a lot more experience and have seen how the world operates. I would rethink my plans.
   b. I'll listen seriously, but they have to show me evidence that they're right.
   c. I'll talk about it with them, but a lot of people don't understand how the world is changing these days. I trust myself to make my own decisions.
   d. They can think what they think. As long as what I'm doing can't cause any kind of permanent damage, I'm going my own way. I have good instincts.

2. Have you found any mentors so far in your life?
   a. I can make it on my own by showing the world what I can do.
   b. I would like a mentor but don't know how to find one.
   c. My bosses at my summer jobs have been good to me, and a few of my teachers are willing to write me good recommendations.
   d. One of my bosses helped me find a great internship and introduced me to friends who are in the industry where I want to make my career.

3. How do you and your friends communicate?
    a. We text.
    b. Group chat.
    c. I try to call them pretty often because we find out more about how we're doing when we're talking.
    d. I love to meet people face-to-face, have them over. My friends aren't just people I communicate with sometimes; we need each other.

4. How often are you in touch with your less-than-closest friends, such as people you met on summer vacation or friends who moved away?
    a. I don't have time to stay in touch much, but I'll respond if they reach out to me.
    b. I follow them on social media and sometimes comment on their posts.
    c. We don't see each other as often as I'd like, but when we do, it's like we were never separated.
    d. I reach out to all my buddies. I'm always interested in what they're up to and I'm always learning new things from them.

5. If something you thought you were going to like—a party, an after-school job, etc.—ends up being boring, what do you do?
    a. I get out of there. I don't have time to waste.
    b. I'll stay long enough not to insult someone at a party or let down a boss.
    c. A good time is always in the eye of the beholder. I'll try to look for what's positive about it.
    d. You can never tell what you'll get out of a new experience. If the party has a bad vibe, maybe I'll go have a talk with a person who's sitting alone looking miserable. If the work is boring, I'll try to figure out a new way of doing the job that's more interesting.

6. How would you describe your feelings about spending time with people?
    a. I really need a lot of alone time. It's just how I'm made.
    b. I have a good time with others, but the experience exhausts me.
    c. I like being with one or two people, not a big group.
    d. I like opportunities to have a lot of good talks and maybe meet some new people.

7. How would you describe your attitude about work?
    a. I want to do a nice, stable job and leave on time.
    b. I would really like to excel at my work and get lots of positive feedback and promotions.
    c. I will pour myself into my work to turn in the most polished product.
    d. I'm always looking for ways to make a school assignment special and give it that extra flair or that little bit of creativity. I need a job that lets me do that, or I'll be bored to tears.

8. How much learning do you do outside your schoolwork?
    a. Having to do all those assignments at school keeps me more than busy enough.
    b. I've been working on learning some kind of new thing, like trying a bunch of different knots.
    c. Most days, I read a book that wasn't assigned by a teacher.
    d. I keep up on current events and look for interesting articles to read on topics that I don't know well.

Scoring: People who decide not to aim for a four-year college in their first several years out of high school are mavericks of a sort. Whether they're doing residential volunteering, working on a farm, studying as an apprentice to get a well-paid job, starting a business, or making a video, they're going against the conventional wisdom that you have to have a bachelor's degree to have a good life. They're less worried about how things look to other people than in doing what feels right to them at the time. Almost invariably, they are also good with people. They make friends and are happy working in groups. As a result, they have a network of people looking out for them, just as they look out for their own friends. And they draw mentors who teach them the ropes, an education they find more useful than school.

They read and stay up on things not because a teacher is making them do it but because they want to keep growing as people. They're the opposite of oblivious, because instead of learning in a classroom, they're learning by living and doing. And because they are willing to go against the grain, they usually are looking for new things to do and new ways to do them; they are not content to plod through life.

Give yourself 1 point for each A answer, 2 for B, 3 for C, 4 for D. A score of 8 to 20 shows that you might have a tough time making it without the formal education of college; a score of 20 to 32 indicates that you have the people skills and willingness to break with the crowd, finding your own road without a bachelor's degree.

FINDING YOUR NATURAL CAREERS

The workplace is a far less stable place than it used to be. The upside is that there's far more freedom and mobility. Employers no longer automatically look askance at workers who have bounced around a bit. People can more easily change the field they're working in.

So don't worry if the first path you choose doesn't work out; as you'll see in the stories of people who didn't go to a four-year college out of high school, they very often started in one thing and then moved to something else, or maybe on to a few different things until they found what worked for them. The same is often true of people who go straight to college; they graduate uncertain of what to do next and try things out. Many of them change direction.

But to get started, it pays to think about what you actually like doing. And that should be based not on what sounds good to you, but on what you actually do, right now. It says something when, with your busy life, you make room for certain interests. So here is a list of activities that should get you thinking about how you like to spend your time.

So, which of these do you like to do? Feel free to add something you do that isn't on this list:

Read
Tell stories
Spend time with children
Play video games, even create games
Participate in sports and athletics
Work in the garden
Fix things
Get involved in politics or social justice issues
Make things out of wood
Program
Draw, paint, or do other artwork
Take care of pets
Work on cars
Sew and knit
Tinker around with graphic design
Write in a journal or write stories or poetry
Do the crossword or other word puzzles
Grow plants including vegetables
Dance
Debate and discuss, especially current events
Cook and/or bake
Make videos
Act or sing
Take photographs
Organize parties and fun events

Play an instrument
Produce music
Build up social media followers
Design clothes
Practice different ways of putting on makeup
Work out
Spend time in nature and learn about it
Help friends and others having problems
Learn new things on YouTube
Run my own little business
Learn languages

Got your items checked off? Now you can search online for the fields and jobs that are heavy on those activities, looking for cross sections. They didn't have an internet to explore when I was getting started, but it didn't take much imagination to link my dual love of writing and constantly learning about entirely new things to the news business. Social media influencers combine their personal interest—whether makeup, dance, a certain heritage, or humor—with their desire to entertain. Combine your answers here with your characteristics from the work style and personality characteristics quizzes—maybe you play around with clothing design, like to make videos, and are mission-driven. Put it all in. See what happens. Again, I find an AI platform to be a particularly user-friendly platform for this; it pulls from multiple sources and will work with as many factors as you ask.

People who play an instrument don't always entertain; in this book, you'll learn about a man whose love of music brought him into the world of managing musicians, music production, and event planning. People who run their own small business in high school could become entrepreneurs, but they're also using skills—getting the word out, organizing their time, pleasing customers, managing money—that easily translate into jobs with large companies, doing consulting, customer service, human resources, marketing, analysis, financial services, and the like.

And when you find some careers that seem of interest, reach out to people who do those things for a living. See if you can spend a day or, even better, a week shadowing them in their jobs. Then you can get a sense of whether this work, as it's practiced in real life, still excites you or whether you had an overly idealized view of it.

As you do all this, think in terms of, as college expert Michael B. Horn said to me, "what brings you energy, what comes easily to you." Work is the place where all the people, with their very different skills, abilities, and interests, find their individual ways to contribute to the world.

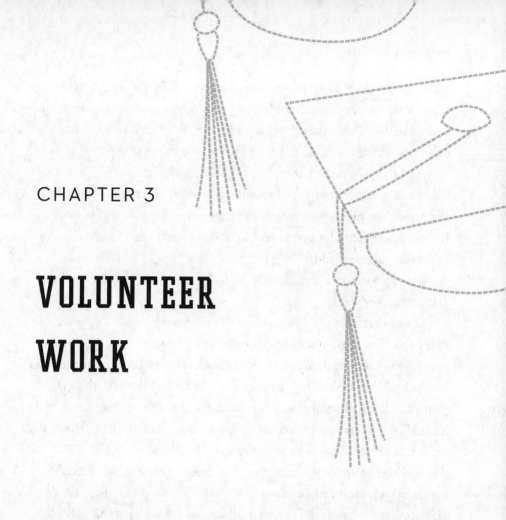

CHAPTER 3

VOLUNTEER WORK

I've been doing volunteer work for years. That's allowed me to become an amateur archaeologist, paleontologist, counselor to teenage girls, and field-trip chaperone to underserved preschoolers who craved outdoor fun. I've delivered supermarkets' donated goods to a food bank and worked in farm fields harvesting vegetables. Almost always, the work has brought me more than I've given. I've learned new skills and new worlds, met people, and enjoyed good times and the satisfaction of doing good for others. But one particular volunteer gig actually changed my life.

I live in a beach town in Southern California that's surrounded by a greenbelt of thousands of acres of wilderness. For a long time, the land was privately owned, closed to the public. I was always wildly curious about what was behind the barbed-wire fences surrounding the land, a holdover from cattle-grazing days. Some people jumped the fences to explore, but as a journalist, I always had to keep in mind how bad it would be to get caught breaking the rules, even if it just involved a wrist-slap.

And then the county opened a big section of that land as a weekend wilderness park. They needed volunteers to meet and greet people, help them plot out hikes, and spread information about safe and respectful hiking. It sounded like a good way to find out more and support the idea of preserving open land.

I took a few hours of minimal training, went on an introductory hike, and was on my way.

Up to that point, I could count the number of trails I'd hiked on one hand. But sitting at the sign-in table also meant I was talking to people who knew a fair amount about the local wilderness and the plants and animals that inhabited these lands. The more I learned, the more I wanted to know. The next step in volunteering was to become a certified naturalist and lead people on interpretive hikes. I would have access to trails that the public was banned from using.

So I signed up for the community college course required for certification, which meant night classes after my day job, plus rising at 4 a.m. on Saturdays to get to the required weekly hikes that began shortly after dawn. The experience was eye-opening. Wild plants especially intrigued me (and, unlike insects and birds, they considerately stayed put while I looked them up in my field guide). I was particularly interested in how Native Americans and white settlers used these plants for food and medicine and in other ways. I learned how the white patches on a cactus can conceal a tiny bug with a brilliant red color. In early North American history, that color, called cochineal, was so treasured for red dye that it rivaled silver in price.

The hikes I led covered the uses of wild plants—and these hikes were so interesting that they led me to join more hikes with knowledgeable people and to yet *another* community college course, this time to become a certified interpretive guide.

But the real change in my life was becoming an avid hiker at the age of forty-eight, treading trails all over the county and everywhere I visited. Hiking became a form of meditation to me, my escape when I was feeling off or discouraged. Over time, it helped shape my identity.

A friend who knew about my passion called to say that a major publisher was looking for someone to write a hiking book about my county for their 50 Hikes in . . . series. Within a couple of months, I had a paying contract to write a book about hiking. The publication of *50 Hikes in Orange County* led to paid speaking engagements and assignments to write magazine articles about hiking and nature in general. I was even offered a job to work as a naturalist at a private reserve, a position I reluctantly turned down to continue my career in journalism. But who knows how my life would have been different if I'd discovered this in my late teens or twenties, instead of in my late forties?

The world needs help, and we have the power to provide it. Volunteer work is a chance to make a difference. But because we enter volunteering to explore and serve rather than to carve out a career, we're naturally more open to new and unexpected experiences that might show us a path forward for our lives—*without* paying a fortune in college tuition and room and board to get to that place. Volunteering teaches you skills and brings new professional contacts into your life. It's often much more interesting than most paid jobs and makes you a more attractive job candidate in the future. Most important, it introduces you to new worlds and new people who are passionate about what they do, and isn't that what you want for your own life?

•

At Camphill Village in Copake, New York—just a few hours outside of New York City—you don't have to pay anything except the fare to get there. Even your medical insurance is covered. In exchange for volunteer service, you receive a private room and board, as well as a stipend of close to $200 a month, plus additional money for travel when it's vacation time.

While there, said Elvira Neal, part of the development team at Copake, you're likely to learn woodworking; organic, biodynamic farming; the making of herbal medicine; commercial baking; and other crafts. You'll also learn to work with developmentally disabled adults in an environment designed to provide them with dignity and security. At the same time, you'll be invited to contribute through creative activities of your own, whether music, writing, or any of your other interests.

Camphill, which has fifteen villages in the United States and even more of them abroad, was created as a way for adults who cannot live independently to spend their lives as an equal part of a community. They participate alongside the volunteers, called coworkers, in making their village run.

The organization's villages give you a chance to travel to places you might otherwise never see and cover all or many of your expenses for the time you choose to stay. Considering that minimum-wage jobs don't come close to providing a living wage, that's not a bad start.

Camphill villages are extraordinary places. In Copake, about 230 residents live and work communally, growing crops, raising farm animals, operating a commercial bakery, making stained glass, and providing a meaningful and dignified life for people with developmental disabilities.

But residential volunteer work extends all over the world and includes unbelievable opportunities. You could be training horses at a rescue ranch (even if you don't know how to ride one); working for social change in Israeli towns; helping to run a hostel in Amsterdam; patrolling the backcountry at a spectacular national park in New Mexico; teaching English in Sudan; or maintaining the Appalachian Trail. You can often extend your volunteer stints or stack different experiences one after the other.

Obviously, no one's going to make a career out of volunteering. Well, almost no one. Elvira Neal is one exception; she has been living at Camphill for a quarter of a century. But these gigs can lead to career opportunities while also providing the opportunity to gain perspective and skills, see new worlds, and put something impressive and unusual on a résumé without the often-prohibitive cost of college.

Among the important things to be learned through volunteering are the so-called soft skills, which refers to the ability to communicate, resolve conflicts, work as part of a team, think critically, and problem-solve creatively. These skills might sound like nothingburgers, but they're highly valued by employers, who complain that far too many job applicants lack them.

The volunteers themselves often agree on that score. "We find when we ask people what they've gotten out of it, it's rarely learning how to run the chainsaw," said Caleb Stevens, recruitment and admissions manager of the Montana Conservation Corps. "It's more like, 'I learned how not to be conflict averse. I learned how to manage risk. How to work in a group environment.'"

Volunteering is also a smart investment because it impresses employers. A 2012 study by the federal government's Corporation for National and Community Service found that people who had engaged in serious volunteer work were 27 percent more likely to be hired for paid jobs.[1] The Center for Economic and Policy Research found that not only were volunteers who put in substantial hours more likely to be hired into paying jobs, but they also tended to be paid more—and who doesn't want that?

Four out of five hiring managers said they're more likely to hire someone with volunteer experience, according to a 2016 study by Deloitte.[2] And they were more willing to overlook other flaws in a résumé if the applicant had been involved in skills-based volunteer work.

At Camphill, volunteers use soft skills on a daily basis. They learn to work with people of all kinds of backgrounds—not just with disabled people but also young people from around the world. About half of the volunteers are international. "Coworkers learn to work through difficult times in a community. They can't just walk away from others," Elvira Neal said. "They have to resolve conflicts."

Camphill got its start in the early 1960s; there are now fifteen villages across the country and many more worldwide, based on the anthroposophist beliefs of Rudolf Steiner, which are also the basis for the Waldorf schools. Everyone is considered a volunteer and equal member of the community, Elvira said. That includes people who have worked there for decades, the disabled residents, and the "coworkers"—mostly young people, largely fresh out of high school, who live there for six months or more, all of them working the farm and in the crafts.

The coworkers interact, live closely with, and assist those who have disabilities. All live in private rooms within communal houses and are provided with food from the village's farm. Learning organic, biodynamic farming practices is part of the experience. Everyone learns to make products for sale in the craft shops—through woodworking, candle-making (with beeswax from the farm's bees), bookbinding, weaving, maple-syrup manufacture, and medicinal herbalism. Sales help support the village. All participate in raising and tending farm animals, milking cows by hand, and learning how to cook nutritious food from scratch.

Volunteers also create new ways of doing things that alleviate routines and bring their own talents to the operation in ways that elevate it to new levels. "There was one young woman writer who taught a weekly poetry-writing class," Elvira told me. "It was extremely popular."

Many volunteers continue to pursue the skills they learned at Camphill after they've left, whether it's operating a snowplow or cooking an inventive vegetarian meal. The daughter of a friend of mine is now working on another farm using sustainable practices. But if you decide that work with developmentally disabled people also provides a meaningful possible life path for you, the organization offers additional opportunities. You could stay an extra year or much longer, or you could attend Camphill Academy, offered at just two US locations, including Copake.

The academy is an accredited college offering a bachelor's degree in three areas—two of them involved in working with developmentally disabled people, which often lead to careers in social work, political advocacy, and other fields. The third is in biodynamic farming. Though there are classes one day a week and a couple of evenings, the education is mostly hands-on, which is a better fit for a lot of students.

And it's free.

Bonus: If you're interested in Camphill, you're not limited to the fifteen locations in the United States. Some thirty more Camphill locations around the world welcome coworkers from this country. Many are located in Europe, but others are in places as varied as Botswana, Vietnam, and Argentina. That gives you the chance to have an international adventure for the cost of flying there while still contributing to others and adding to your skill set.

•

I developed a kinship with nature through volunteering later in life. But if you've been drawn to the pull of the wild from a young age, know that you don't need a college degree to get a career start in conservation. The Montana Conservation Corps (MCC), which helps preserve wild areas in a wide variety of ways, accepts high school grads—or those with a GED—for service periods that last from three to ten months.

You might be doing anything from weeding out invasive plants to restoring the natural landscape to reaching out to visitors. You may be camping in areas of Yellowstone National Park where the public isn't even allowed to wander. Caleb Stevens, MCC recruitment and admissions manager, says he works to match volunteers' individual interests with their assignments. Care about animal wildlife? You could be assigned to help beaver populations, which have been found key to reducing wildfire damage. If wildfire ecology is your interest, you might be mentored by an expert in that field. Working on climate change issues is another, newer option. You might end up craving a future in environmental work, or simply want to build the depth of your knowledge about nature.

Conservation work can be physically taxing, but for those who love camping or outdoor adventures, it can also be heavenly. Field crews often camp out in backcountry that is beyond the standard, crowded tourist offerings while they work on their projects. They get to see and experience the wilderness in ways that few people do—all under expert supervision.

The corps doesn't create the dormitory-like setting of a place like

Camphill but does provide various forms of financial help. To start with, there's a stipend that starts at more than $600 every two weeks, depending on the work involved, in addition to a daily food allowance. Free training is provided. Regular housing is not provided, but time spent camping during field work is rent-free.

Most recently, the corps has been pairing host families with many of its five hundred or so volunteers each year. Those families provide a room for very little money and often for free as a kindness to the workers. The corps also connects volunteers with each other so they can find group rentals, which generally works out to significantly less money per person.

Conservation corps work goes back to the New Deal of the 1930s, when it got its start as a program to help lift the nation out of depression. But the modern program—in its expanded and evolved form—began in 1985. The Montana corps is one of 140 conservation corps nationwide, and though there's some variation in how they're run, many (including the Montana corps) are affiliated with AmeriCorps, the federal volunteering program. This means that you're eligible for not just the stipend of the corps you choose but also some of the benefits of AmeriCorps—such as free health insurance and education grants of up to $7,000 or so for college or any other kind of formal training you might want afterward.

The many conservation corps are all grouped under an umbrella organization of twenty-five thousand volunteers nationwide called the Corps Network, which offers a tremendous choice of environment and location, including Hawaii and Alaska. Some corps organizations in warm-weather areas take volunteers for yearlong stints and offer additional scholarships. California alone has more than twenty corps organizations. The Montana corps covers parks, wilderness, and open land throughout Montana, Idaho, Wyoming, and North and South Dakota, giving you a wide range of choice in both location and assignment. If you want a longer and broader experience, you can even stack assignments, one after another.

All the conservation corps can be accessed through the Corps Network (corpsnetwork.org), where you can hunt around on the individual websites for places and assignments that most interest you.

Volunteers who join the corps as a break from college often find that they return to school with a better sense of direction and a new ability to manage challenges. Sage Breck of Colorado is in her second year of conservation corps work, after finishing high school at the age of seventeen. After stints building trails amid the dramatic scenery of Arapaho and Roosevelt National Forests in Colorado and restoring land to its natural state at Walker Basin Conservancy in Nevada, she's moved on to forest thinning to minimize wildfire damage with the Montana Conservation Corps. She's also received her certification as a Class A sawyer (somebody who saws timber for a living).

Sage was provided with extremely low-cost housing—no more than $200 a month—and a monthly living stipend of about $600. In Montana, though, she camps out of her small SUV in a backcountry campsite with other volunteers, who cook together and watch out for each other, in an area that's not open to the public.

Once her forestry work is over, Sage wants to attend college. But her work in the wilderness has changed her. She's developed a more focused eye on her studies, but at the same time, she's pulled out of the rat-race view of life.

"I'm just a lot more open-minded and relaxed about not being on a very specific agenda," Sage said. "Maybe I change majors or change colleges, it's no big deal."

And she definitely wants to study ecology in some form, perhaps wildlife biology. "I've homed in on exactly what I want that to look like," she said. "I want a job where I can be outdoors doing field research. And also making a change environmentally. This work has invigorated that passion."

But the best parts of her conservation work, she said, were the more personal aspects.

"It enabled me to develop resilience, the ability to deal with anything and go with the flow," she said. "Plus, I've made really great connections with a huge and diverse range of people."

Though the conservation corps have a far greater number of

residential volunteer opportunities, the National Park Service offers plenty of short-term service work for people who live near one of the country's four hundred parks—all of which need help. In fact, it's estimated that the parks' nearly three hundred thousand volunteers donate about six million hours of service each year.

To find out about opportunities, contact your nearest national parks. If you're looking for residential stints, however, which might include bunkhouses or cabins or give you a campsite or RV pad, use the centralized internet site volunteer.gov. It's not specific to the park service, but the site's filters make it the easiest way to search for the work you might want to do and includes some other agencies that do similar work. Keep in mind that the big-name parks such as Yosemite get the most applications; to increase your chances, give some of the smaller parks a look. Type "housing" in the search field to bring up any opportunities that offer some kind of free housing (the Park Service does not provide food or a stipend). This will narrow your search and allow you to check out each job to see if it meets your interests.

Volunteer opportunities are also available at national forests, wildlife preserves, and state and regional parks. In my California county, park ranger reserves serve in our many regional and wilderness parks. Often, these volunteers work their way up to full-time ranger jobs at regional and wilderness parks by taking a set of courses at a local community college.

•

The federal volunteer system AmeriCorps is mostly known as something people do right after college. In fact, only about a third of AmeriCorps volunteers are college graduates. Another third have some college behind them, and a third are high school grads with no college, according to Sonali Nijhawan, director of AmeriCorps State and National, which funds many of the organizations that employ volunteers.

Aside from awarding grants, AmeriCorps is split into two main programs. In the National Civilian Community Corps (NCCC), teams of volunteers travel the nation as needed. They might help new immigrants at refugee camps or aid communities after natural disasters. They build housing for low-income people and help run community fundraisers. Some served as volunteers at COVID-19 vaccination clinics when the vaccine became available. Terms of service might be for a summer, ten months, or a full year, and each tenure may involve several different tasks. Room, board, and travel from assignment to assignment are covered, but the short-term work sometimes means that lodging might be military barracks or churches filled with cots.

In addition to their keep, NCCC volunteers receive free health insurance and an education grant to help with future college or technical school education. They're paid a stipend of a minimum of $6,700 for a ten-month tour of duty as well.

NCCC work can be arduous. You might end up with assignments that trouble you, such as helping organizations with a political or religious bent that run counter to your beliefs. Consider that a chance to practice your tolerance, as well as see the country, get to know people from very different backgrounds, and live independently from home— plus accomplish some important work.

Kay Gardner was in college but hadn't completed her degree when she went looking for meaningful work that didn't require a bachelor's. She signed up for a stint in AmeriCorps' NCCC. For her last project she was stationed in Paradise, California, helping to provide relief to the local community after the deadly Camp Fire of 2018. The project lasted three months. Kay's team worked in weed abatement to create fire-safe properties, served weekly community dinners to the residents of Paradise, engaged at local goods-distribution centers, built tiny homes for fire survivors, "and so much more," Kay told the career center when she returned to Arizona State University. Working with the NCCC, Kay said, had been the "best decision of my life."

Volunteers who work for VISTA, AmeriCorps' second main program, tend to work on larger-scale efforts such as environmental projects or helping local nonprofits bring in more funding through grant applications and development work, even if they have no experience in that. VISTA often places volunteers directly in impoverished areas, where they stay through their service term, usually ten months. The program works best for self-starters who can take on learning about complex tasks that might be entirely new to them.

Room and board aren't provided, though VISTA gives volunteers a bigger living allowance than NCCC members receive: $17,600 and up a year, depending on the cost of living where they're serving. Otherwise, VISTA provides the same benefits—education awards and health insurance—as the NCCC. While NCCC members can work an unlimited number of terms but must take breaks from service after no more than two terms in a row, VISTA volunteers can serve for up to five straight years. But a main complaint of many VISTA volunteers is that without housing opportunities, the living allowance isn't nearly enough. They're basically living close to the poverty line—the same one they're trying to eradicate—which AmeriCorps considers beneficial to the experience. "The stipend enables you to live very frugally, like the community you are serving," wrote Sarah Westbrook, VISTA's marketing coordinator in 2017.[3]

AmeriCorps often touts its hiring pipelines, which give volunteers priority for many paid federal jobs. In addition, about six hundred companies, nonprofits, and local government agencies have signed on to give AmeriCorps alums a leg up on hiring after their service has ended. These include Accenture, Comcast, and the American Red Cross. Some of the program's alumni say, though, that it hasn't given them a leg up on employment.

Then there's Mario Fedelin, who turned his stint with AmeriCorps into much more: a mission for his life, a nonprofit of his own, and a good living as well.

When he first signed up, Mario wasn't really thinking about six-figure salaries or a future as an executive. He mainly was trying to figure out how to leave his job as a barista. He'd been rejected by the colleges where he'd applied, and he'd worked multiple jobs, often at the same time, that didn't pay very well and weren't meaningful to him. He had just returned to his hometown of San Jose, thinking of working his way through community college.

But then, walking through the city's downtown at age twenty, Mario saw a group of young adults wearing familiar yellow jackets—the regulation uniform of City Year workers.

City Year is a program of AmeriCorps, the national umbrella organization of many public service groups. At the time, its main mission was to develop leadership know-how among teenagers.

Mario knew those yellow jackets from a week in the woods he had spent at Camp Anytown with a cross section of many different kinds of kids learning about leadership. There he met a City Year volunteer who had great passion for his work and whom Mario saw as being full of joy—the kind of life he wanted to live. Not only that, he said this volunteer "looked like me"—a young Latino man.

So when he saw the yellow jackets, Mario felt inspired and walked into the recruiting office of AmeriCorps.

Mario's City Year work involved leadership classes for kids on Saturdays. He was paid a stipend that covered his living expenses, but more important, the work gave him a taste of where his skills lay. "I felt like a natural at it," he said. After a couple of years, he was invited to take a leadership position with AmeriCorps in Philadelphia.

He then returned to California and worked on ways to reduce dropout rates in the high schools and help more underrepresented kids get into college—but as a manager, conferring with school principals and helping AmeriCorps volunteers work with students. His teams ran after-school programs and recreational events.

But Mario was more drawn to youth leadership, especially when kids came to him with service projects they wanted to carry out. They needed someone to cut red tape for them and help them learn how to turn their ambitions into reality.

So in 2015, he and a friend created a new nonprofit, Changeist, working with kids as young as eleven from all kinds of neighborhoods, rich and poor, trying to create solutions for more affordable housing and take on other social and economic problems in the region. They learn public speaking, social engagement, and how to carry out service projects in their communities, which have included a community garden and sourcing and creating hygiene kits for the unhoused. A $1.8 million investment came in 2018 from the State of California; the group's work was recognized by the Obama Foundation. Now in his early forties, Mario lives in the Los Angeles area. In 2022, his salary was in the six figures, and he is CEO of his own operation, doing what matters most to him, all without a college degree.

"I waited for a long time to build my civic home," he said. "We wanted something to build that earlier in young people."

•

Since 2017, Candida "Candy" Haasch has brought residential volunteers to her horse rescue, Warriors of the Rainbow Horse Sanctuary. This isn't a scut work job mucking out stalls; the horses are in pastures. Most of it involves training the horses to become calm, people-trusting riding steeds. Of course, there's also grooming and simple health-maintenance work.

It doesn't matter if you know nothing about the specialized skill of training horses or don't even know how to ride them. Many of Candy's volunteers have extensive experience riding, but some, she said, hardly know the head from the tail. No matter. Volunteers are trained along with the horses and housed for free in the camper on the nineteen-acre property or in one of the bedrooms of Candy's house. They're not paid a stipend or provided with health insurance, but they're expected to give only twenty hours of work each week. If you have a car, you could look for a part-time job in the area to subsidize your volunteer gig. There are also plenty of opportunities to ride in a beautiful nearby conservation area and to become an accomplished rider at the arena of a local board member.

Most volunteers—Candy usually has more than one at a time—stay for a few months or a half year, but they're welcome to stay longer. Many return for additional stints.

In addition to learning the specialized skill of training horses, volunteers gain experience in taking control of situations that might seem daunting. Horses don't always take amiably to training; the volunteers learn how to overcome their fears and take the lead in the human-horse relationship without the use of harsh measures and build an affectionate and cooperative kinship with the animals. It's a skill that will serve them well with future bosses, employees, and, for that matter, kids of their own who are forever testing the limits.

Many animal sanctuaries rely on volunteer work. When you find one you like, it's imperative you do your research. Confirm that it's a solid and respected (and officially registered) nonprofit, operated in a way that's safe for you. (We all watched *Tiger King*, right?) Do a little online sleuthing. Has the sanctuary been in the news? Are there any online reviews? Contact alums to get their take. And avoid sanctuaries that charge you money for volunteering.

On the nonresidential front, zoos usually are looking for volunteers. At the Smithsonian's National Zoo in Washington, DC, aides help with animal care, science, and other behind-the-scenes activities. Volunteer interpreters help educate the public about the animals and conservation.

•

When it's time to start searching on your own, think about what kind of work most interests you and where you'd like to be, and hunt online for opportunities. I've always been intrigued by archaeology and paleontology. Most of the work in these disciplines makes the volunteer pay for the privilege—often, quite a bit. But I found digs in my county that took beginners like me and trained us, as well as an inexpensive Arizona dude ranch that allows guests to volunteer at its archaeological site for a nominal fee. The county I live in also has a vast warehouse of six million fossils and archaeological artifacts; whenever developers come across those finds, they're required to have them properly excavated and sent to the warehouse, which enlists volunteers to sort and prepare the specimens. I spent one evening using a tiny electric drill bit to clean prehistoric whale vertebrae, millions of years old, of their hardened crust of rock and sand.

If you search around, you can find more distant and long-term possibilities. The Dickinson Museum Center in North Dakota, for example, which includes the Badlands Dinosaur Museum, sponsors summer digs of dinosaur bones. The environment is primitive—you're tent camping for weeks—but it's free, and so is the food that volunteers take turns cooking. If you're looking to volunteer your hard labor without paying for the privilege, Amanda Hendrix, collections manager and museum educator at the Badlands museum, suggests checking out natural history museums, which seldom require any payment. Those are also great places to volunteer in paleontology or archaeology laboratories.

You may be seeking volunteer opportunities with a spiritual bent. Religious retreat centers—Buddhist, Hindu, Christian, and so forth— are a popular option that often includes room and board as well as training. Many are located in beautiful settings and allow volunteers to be part of the larger community.

The Vedanta Spiritual and Holistic Retreat Center in the community of California Hot Springs, amid the Sierra Foothills bordering Sequoia National Park, focuses on panreligious spirituality. Volunteers who are willing to give at least four weeks of service (though it encourages a lot more; one volunteer I talked to has been there for seven years) at thirty hours a week might do organic farming, landscaping, mural painting, creative projects, and small-scale construction. In exchange, they are given a campsite to live at and meals as well as access to daily yoga practice and use of the land.

There are several free, legitimate, centralized websites to help you find volunteer work. The best are VolunteerMatch and Idealist.

But if you're looking for something suited especially to you, dig a little deeper. A search engine ultimately is your best guide to finding meaningful work. Plug in the areas of the world and the kind of work you're interested in, along with the phrase "residential volunteer opportunities." Or just start making calls. Think of ways you might be able to help an organization and make a pitch to them about how you are willing to contribute and/or what you could accomplish.

Avoid sites that require you to go through them to find these opportunities; these almost always charge significant money and are more like travel agencies than volunteer agencies. It's your work and caring that these organizations should want, not your money.

•

Destiny Saturria wanted something more meaningful for her life than just a drudge job, but she had no idea what that might be. She found the answer through volunteering at a Camphill farm and village for the developmentally disabled.

It sounded different from her life in Miami. She learned about baking and farming and caring for those unable to care for themselves. She turned into an avid reader with many interests and a new sense of direction and purpose.

But what struck me the most, talking with her, was the sense of peace and joy in her words and voice.

That's a big change from the teenager who dropped out of her Miami high school, hampered in her studies by ADHD and feeling as though she simply didn't belong. But she also knew she had things to learn about living a worthwhile adult life.

"I always had in my mind that I wanted to do something more than just everyday fast food and waitressing jobs," she says.

With a yearning to see more of the world after living in Miami her whole life, but without the credentials or financial resources to head out traveling or looking for a job, she plugged the words "volunteer work" and "live-in position" into her search engine.

That's how she arrived in Copake, New York, a couple of hours out of New York City, where she became one of the community's coworkers, or residential volunteers. There she was provided with a private room and meals, as well as health insurance and a small stipend. After stints working with disabled elderly people and learning how to bake in the farm's commercial bakery, she missed the outdoors and switched to working five and a half hours a day in the vegetable garden of Camphill's biodynamic farm, six days a week, and still helping out the community's elderly residents. The seventh day was for resting or heading to the city for fun with some of the other volunteers. In her downtime, she joined a group that does a type of expressive body movement called eurhythmics, and involved herself in arts, crafts, and reading.

Destiny originally figured she could stick out six months at Camphill. Instead, she stayed two years. "I fell in love with the village in general and the life, the sharing and open communities."

She also met her romantic partner there. But the biggest changes have been internal.

"It's made me realize the world does not revolve around just us," she said. "It's changed how I communicate; you're not just thinking about your life but the lives of others."

Growing her own food and cooking from scratch also led her to healthier eating habits. "It makes you think about how you eat and what you're feeding others." She learned about herbal medicine.

"I think if I never came to the village, I would be lost on what my future would be," she said.

She has a much better idea now: working with the elderly, which she wants to do as a private caregiver.

"There's something about caring for someone and seeing their smile after, their looks and the appreciation in their eyes. I would love to be giving more to others."

She's aiming to work in a Spanish-speaking home in Latin America, preferably in the Dominican Republic.

"I am Puerto Rican and Dominican," she said. "I speak Spanish but not enough to talk about politics. So, I would love to really be able to speak the language completely and get a feeling for my culture." Gaining a language would also help her find future jobs; multilingualism is in demand.

But Camphill will forever be a part of who she is. "This is a dream place. You work like anyone else, but you always have backup. No one ever forces you when you feel you're working too hard and too stressed, and that's not what the real world would say."

The world back in Miami is far more fast-paced and money-oriented, but Destiny's chosen to be a lifelong learner, a woman who feels calm, fulfilled, and ready to contribute to the world.

FINDING THE GOOD VOLUNTEER WORK

The work that nonprofits do can be life- and world-changing. But even in this field, there are groups and people who are less than totally altruistic. Protect yourself in looking for good volunteer stints. Of course, the big ones such as the conservation corps are going to be legit. But for organizations you've never heard of, there could be people looking to take your money, living or working conditions that are unsafe or unacceptable, or work that does nothing to meet your desire to learn, contribute, or find out more about the world and your place in it.

I had originally planned to include in this chapter a very remote retreat center that sounded beautiful. But as I looked into it more, I found some negative reviews and allegations of barbed-wire fencing, big guard dogs, and keeping out the public that made me uncomfortable enough to exclude it, though if carefully checked out in person, it could prove to be a good spot for the right volunteers.

So remember: Don't just take a website's word for anything if you don't know the organization. Do your due diligence when it comes to research to ensure a nonprofit looks legit:

- Check for reviews of the places where you're looking to volunteer.
- Make sure the organization is registered as a nonprofit (they should be able to provide you with tax forms that show it).
- Do an online search for any negative (or positive) articles written about them; the local newspaper is also a good place to do a search.

- If you can, visit the place beforehand and ask to meet volunteers—unchaperoned by supervisors who might inhibit what they'll say—to find out about their experiences.
- Beware any "volunteer" work that has you paying for tuition, training, or a place to stay. You shouldn't have to pay anything beyond the cost of getting there, perhaps your health insurance, and in some cases your food.

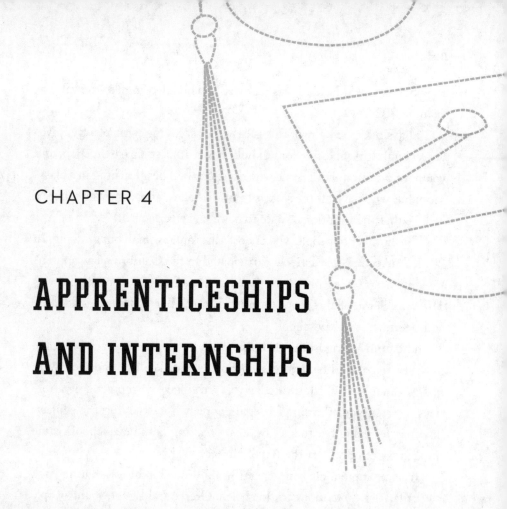

CHAPTER 4

APPRENTICESHIPS AND INTERNSHIPS

Kim Kardashian: celebrity and . . . the most famous apprentice in the country.

As all apprentices do, this California resident is using her practical training to pursue an additional career. But in this case, she's doing it to become a lawyer.

California is one of four states (the others are Vermont, Virginia, and Washington) where you don't have to go to law school or get a bachelor's degree to become a lawyer. Instead, you study under a practicing lawyer or judge for four years and, in California, pass a first-year exam known as the baby bar. Ultimately, you're allowed to take the full bar exam, which, if you pass, entitles you to be a lawyer the same as a graduate of Stanford

Law School. (Kardashian was reportedly scheduled to take the full bar exam in 2024.)

That's not to say any of this is easy. But studying with a lawyer gives you enough time and freedom to hold down at least a part-time job, and you pay no tuition. For people who don't do their best learning in a classroom but who have all the smarts to practice law, apprenticeship offers a chance that the traditional route to being a lawyer cuts off.

The number of people who choose this route is small but growing. In 2015, fourteen people actively participated in the California law apprenticeship program, according to the State Bar. By 2022, the number was 110. And some of the people admitted to the bar had never graduated college, much less law school.

The funny thing is, this is pretty much how *everyone* used to become a lawyer. In colonial America, few people attended college and there were no law schools. Instead, future lawyers "read law" with practicing attorneys, carrying out the simpler legal chores while studying the subject. Thomas Jefferson became a lawyer by reading law. Law schools came into existence only after the Revolutionary War.

In fact, apprenticing in general has a venerable history dating back more than one thousand years. In ancient Greece and Egypt, young people learned their future occupations through the guidance of skilled mentors— journeymen—until they were ready to work without supervision.

Apprenticeship training has continued to this day in the manual trades (see chapter 9), but over the years, white-collar jobs increasingly required college degrees. At least, that's what happened in the United States—Jefferson himself was a proponent of formal law study and funded a law professorship in 1779. But some other countries have been smarter about realizing the value of apprenticeship.

The good news is that apprenticeships are making a big comeback in the United States, with a growing list of organizations and companies setting up these paid trainee programs.

•

A random conversation with a relative introduced me to the concept of white-collar apprenticing. My brother-in-law had a friend who lived in Switzerland; her daughter had apprenticed to become a hotel manager, without needing to attend college. She worked at a hotel part-time while attending high school part-time and then underwent a year of full-time training following graduation—after which she was ready to start her career.

It can be a good job, hotel management. It generally takes place in nice surroundings, doing interesting work with people who are looking for a happy experience. The field is growing, and the median salary is in the low six figures. To do that job in the United States typically requires a bachelor's degree, and it helps to have a master's degree in hospitality.

The Swiss system works like this: Though a large number of students enter the nation's rigorous university system, the country also has a robust educational plan for the many others who aren't college-bound. During their final years of high school, these students attend classes part-time and have part-time, paid apprenticeships in their chosen field. At the end of school, they might or might not need an extra year of training before they start well-paid careers.

If we operated more as the Swiss do, people would save years and many thousands of dollars preparing for the same career.

Even better, high school students learn early in the process whether the field they're interested in is actually the right one for them.

This doesn't just pertain to the hospitality industry. There are loads of professional, white-collar jobs in Switzerland that people train for by apprenticing in high school. University is required for certain careers: doctors, teachers, engineers, and the like. But Swiss students have access to plenty of other interesting careers with good futures—banking, customer service, human resources, data analysis, and so forth—without having to take the country's very challenging pre-college courses and then spending years in post–high school education.

That conversation with my brother-in-law stuck with me, and a couple of years later, I wrote a column about it for the *Sacramento Bee*. I contacted a few parents in Switzerland, all of them expatriate Americans. The Swiss system wasn't perfect, they said, but they preferred it by far over the US system, where bachelor's degrees were required for jobs that didn't seem to need them. One of the women said that her Swiss husband had been a bank executive without a college degree for fifteen years. At that point, he decided to enter university—not because he needed more skills or information but because he feared his credentials wouldn't count for anything with the US bankers with whom he had begun to work.

A few years later, I wrote about Swiss apprenticeships again, this time in an essay for the *Los Angeles Times* that particularly looked at "degree inflation" in the United States—companies requiring bachelor's degrees for jobs that hadn't needed them before and shouldn't need them now. The essay mentioned a Harvard Business School report that found that degree inflation hurt many Americans' ability to enter well-paid careers and also harmed employers because college grads were less likely to stay for long. Anyone, college grad or not, needs training to do specific jobs. Rapid turnover means having to find and train new people all the time. That's not just time-consuming and expensive, but it also means the company is often short on trained people with real experience on the job.

The hiring and retention problem was exacerbated by the COVID-19 pandemic, which resulted in a labor shortage. There were fewer college grads for businesses to hire. At the same time, the Black Lives Matter movement made employers realize they had to stop paying lip service to building a diverse workforce and making incremental improvements. They had to create a more realistic pipeline for hiring white-collar employees.

And increasingly, they're recognizing that apprenticeships are a great way to find, train, and hire their employees of the future.

•

Noel Ginsburg is determined to bring Switzerland to America.

It turns out I wasn't the only one thinking about the Swiss apprenticeship program and how much saner it could be for a lot of Americans.

Ginsburg, the founder of a plastics business in Denver, had been invited on a trip to see how the education system worked in the European country. He had long been interested in providing pathways to the middle class for disadvantaged youth; he previously had promised college scholarships to large numbers of elementary school students, to encourage them to plan early to go to college and not worry that lack of money would stand in their way. Ninety percent of them attended and graduated, he said.

He also had become a believer in the same thing that makes the Swiss system work: that employers couldn't leave everything to schools. They needed to step up and participate in the training that young people would need to embark on careers with a real future. The trip to Europe inspired him.

"I found myself believing by the third day that the solution they had in Switzerland was the solution I was looking for," he told me. "Seventy percent of their students complete an apprenticeship in which their starting salary out of high school is $50,000 to $55,000." He noted that the president of UBS, a vast investment bank based in Switzerland, had started out as an apprentice without a degree and only later attended university.

Ginsburg persuaded the governor of Colorado to lead a contingent of business and education leaders to Switzerland to see how well it worked. And then he started a nonprofit called CareerWise to bring the Swiss system to Denver. Several Denver-area public high schools participate: Courses are arranged so that juniors and seniors can take all their core classes on two or three days a week. On the other days, students work at approved, paid apprenticeships and are usually hired by the same companies when they graduate high school and complete the program. CareerWise acts as the intermediary and support organization.

"Students get [academic] credit for work-based learning," Ginsburg said. "They graduate on time." And the apprenticeships often have a positive effect on their academics. "Once they're in a professional environment and see why math is important, they pay more attention in the classroom."

Early on, Ginsburg asked an official at a Denver-based insurance company, Pinnacol Assurance, whether they hired people without bachelor's degrees for various white-collar jobs. The official said no—but the company was open to hearing Ginsburg's philosophy and acting on it. Now, at least 5 percent of Pinnacol's workforce is made up of youth apprentices working in such fields as insurance underwriting. Another apprentice worked at a bank through the CareerWise program and immediately became a banker with that company.

All the CareerWise apprenticeships must be for white-collar jobs in careers that pay enough to support a family. Ginsburg doesn't want the program to become a way of shunting Black and Latino students into blue-collar jobs, which schools have a long record of doing. Other fields the apprentices enter include business services, marketing, human resources, coding, network support, advanced manufacturing, accounting, and hotel and restaurant management.

CareerWise expanded into New York City in 2021 and in 2022 boasted a cohort of some one thousand apprentices—a number Ginsburg expected to double in the next year. The plan is that CareerWise will eventually become a robust, nationwide program.

It's not that Ginsburg has turned against college. Quite the opposite. He just feels that once students find themselves working real jobs, they'll have a better idea of whether they want college later on. They'll be able to save up money for tuition. And many of them now work for companies that provide tuition reimbursement to employees who continue their education.

"People are rethinking everything about education and the workplace," he said.

•

Gabriella Ayala spent her youngest years stressed about finances in a household that had little money. Qualifying for free and reduced-price meals at school was a major relief. "Because of that, I didn't have to worry about food," she said.

She also had goals and a big interest in computer science and engineering that started in middle school when she bought a used computer. She wanted to take the robotics class her school offered, but the class had too few seats for too many students. She couldn't afford the cost of learning robotics elsewhere, not to mention the price of equipment.

"So I looked around at what was free, and Codeacademy came up on my search list." She started learning computer languages on her own via the website. "I ended up trying to make a little personal diary using the languages. It looked pretty bad, but I'm still proud of it. I wish I had saved it."

If an online robotics class was too pricey, though, affording college was an even bigger obstacle. Luckily for Gabriella, her high school was part of the CareerWise apprenticeship program, and her vice principal suggested she apply.

At first, she went to school three days a week and worked at her technology apprenticeship job at Pinnacol Assurance two days a week. She spent more time in the office and took the community college classes she needed. Her apprenticeship paid minimum wage in the beginning, but she was able to earn regular wage increases over time.

Having an apprenticeship often requires earning certification in certain skills. Gabriella was able to take an online coding camp led by a Pinnacol employee. And she remembers how helpful it was to have mentors guiding her through problems and teaching her different approaches throughout.

Gabriella took her high school diploma in June 2019 and was hired on to Pinnacol that fall as a software engineer specializing in website functionality, with a big increase in pay. By age twenty-one, in 2022, she was earning a six-figure salary. It has enabled a whole new way of life, including paying for a therapist to treat her continued anxiety about money. Even her robust earnings couldn't overcome the childhood stress. But the therapist has helped her realize she's financially stable now.

"It is mind-boggling, especially now that I can buy things," Gabriella said. "I was able to buy my grandparents' house and do a lot of house renovations."

She takes her ten-year-old brother to school each day and plans to urge him to follow her into the apprenticeship route. She thinks he'll listen. "I know I am a model for my little brother."

Her job is fulfilling as well. "This work excites me because it's always challenging. I'll be banging my head against the wall and then have the huge satisfaction of solving the problem. There's nothing like it.

"I'm always learning, which is my favorite part."

Gabriela thinks about what her life would have been like at age twenty-one if she'd chosen college straight out of high school. "I would have still been in college with a lot of student debt and not a lot of income." Given the ups and downs of the tech market—boom hiring that can quickly turn into massive layoffs—she might have had trouble paying off those loans.

Her ambitions haven't ended. She'd like to attend community college and pursue a degree in computer technology. "Eventually I want to go back and get some of those skills and the algorithmic thinking that is helpful in my field," Gabriella said. It helps a lot that Pinnacol has a tuition reimbursement program, though the upfront costs of college remain an impediment.

But so far, she is kicking it in a male-dominated field and notes that the robotics class she missed out on in middle school was predominantly made up of boys. "I'm still a little salty about not being allowed into that robotics class," she said. College would give her a second chance.

For now, Gabriella is astonished to find herself where she is at such a young age: A homeowner with a growing savings account. A mainstay of her family. An experienced professional at age twenty-one.

"The hardest part is not getting a huge ego," she said. "I want to stay humble."

•

When Lanna Hernandez was a sophomore in high school, she went to her school counselor for guidance about her next steps in life.

"At the time, I wanted to get into journalism, but I was just kind of lost on how to get from school to a professional setting," Lanna said. "She showed me the CareerWise program and said it would be a really good fit for me."

Lanna then met with CareerWise counselors, who laid out the list of fields she could enter through the program. She chose marketing and communications, the field most closely aligned with journalism.

Like most apprentices in the program, she started out going to school three days a week and work two days a week, receiving school credit and $14.75 an hour for her office work. She was provided with training in management and marketing, and she earned three certifications.

"CareerWise paid for the trainings," she said. "They gave me notebooks, laptop, anything I needed."

Lanna's goal was to graduate early so she could get a head start on her career. In 2021, she got her high school diploma after less than four years of study. "I could not have done it without the apprenticeship program," she said. "They offered me credits and a lot of support, as well as more education and hands-on experience."

After that, the eighteen-year-old became a full-time marketing coordinator for CareerWise. She drafts emails, updates the website, and writes blog posts. She makes $18 an hour but knows that raises are in her future. She also helps plan and carry out the organization's events.

"It's the kind of job I would have gotten right out of college except I don't have the debt," Lanna said. "I have the credibility of someone who got out of college by doing the same role I do in the office and accomplishing the same thing. I was tired of following the path that everyone else was.

"It's funny because I was very set on going to college," Lanna said. "but once I entered the CareerWise program, I saw there was so much power being given to the youth."

The program showed her how successful she could be in a short time. "It was terrific to learn that if I put my mind to it, I could do anything. It's important to trust your path. Now is the time to learn." For Lanna, that includes studying for her real estate license while she's working.

While Lanna was fully launched on her career, her peers were just starting college.

"My friends and I talk about it all the time," she said. "Since it was different from the traditional route, they didn't really trust it. When I told them about it, they kind of blew it off. Now that I tell them what I'm doing and how I'm succeeding, they're saying, 'Wow, this is such a great opportunity. I wish I had taken it.'"

•

Talking to the people who run the large and growing apprenticeship program at Aon is like reading the Harvard Business School report on why companies shouldn't require bachelor's degrees if the jobs can be performed well without a four-year college education.

Aon, which provides business services to companies, found that college graduates tended to move on from those jobs, said Francheska Feliciano, director of apprenticeship for the company's US headquarters in Chicago. Hiring and training new people is an expensive proposition, and it also means that employees are perpetually less experienced. In addition, Aon and its clients were looking to create a more diverse workplace even as Black and Latino applicants were less likely to have had the opportunity to attend college. That meant offering opportunities and training to people without a bachelor's degree.

The Aon program, begun in 2017 at its US headquarters in Chicago, works differently from high school–based apprenticeships. Applicants must have completed high school or have an equivalency degree; they then apprentice while attending community college in business, working toward an associate's degree. They're paid $45,000 a year during the apprenticeship, which helps them get through their two years of study. Then they receive raises that are gauged to be competitive with the market.

In many ways, Aon fulfills the same role as CareerWise in Denver and New York. It helps companies set up and run apprenticeship programs, and it sets standards for the quality of those apprenticeships. As with CareerWise, this means that apprentices earn certification in their fields of work, as a way of ensuring that they are receiving real training.

In 2019, Aon began expanding the apprentice program to companies across the nation. By 2022, there were about one thousand apprentices across 160 employers, which were required to commit to hiring the apprentices who successfully complete the program.

"We decided to clear out the four-year degree [requirement]," said Shantenae Robinson, who oversees the nationwide apprentice program. "We do the earn-and-learn model to help bring in talent, and it has been super successful."

The goal is to have ten thousand apprentices across ten cities working in such fields as IT, human resources, finance, marketing, research and development, and retail. The field of health care was added in the Houston area in 2023.

·

Juawana Allen was a full-time student at Harold Washington College, part of the Chicago community colleges, majoring in history and minoring in public relations.

"A class was canceled," she said. "I went to the library waiting for my next class to begin, and I saw this flyer for the Aon apprentice program. I asked more about it and filed an application."

She entered the program in 2018, working on insurance plans that help clients insure specific assets or risks, such as being protected against the costs of wildfire and insuring a fleet of trucks. "I learned how to read contracts and work in Excel," she said. "I developed presentation skills."

She was skeptical at first about being trained and getting paid while going to school. It seemed almost too good to be real.

But it was real. And in 2020, when the apprenticeship ended, Juawana, then in her early twenties, was hired full-time as an insurance analyst.

"Instead of background work, I was able to have a seat at the table in terms of my accounts. I was helping to determine the clients' needs and what should be done to meet them."

She then transferred to another team that deals with another type of insurance. Her job is located in New York City, and when we talked in late 2022, she was excited about the new life she would have, moving to Brooklyn.

●

These are a couple of examples of well-run apprenticeships, but where can you find out about apprenticeships in your area and/or field of interest?

It almost always starts with a good internet search. Use the word "apprenticeship" and the field you're interested in entering, or the state where you live. Most states have apprenticeship websites within their departments of education; unfortunately, many of these lack real guidance or detail. But as the popularity of apprenticeships grows, states are likely to put more emphasis on putting out useful information.

The federal government has its own, more detailed website where you can search for available apprenticeships, sorted according to the fields of work that interest you. Try entering several different kinds of jobs—cybersecurity, financial services, insurance, childcare, education, health. Be aware that although many of the jobs listed are professional—i.e., white-collar—the site also includes jobs in the trades that might interest you. Start out at apprenticeship.gov/finder.

Included in this chapter is a partial list of the 160 companies that have begun offering apprenticeships through Aon networks. You can get more complete information by contacting the partner community colleges that work with the companies on their programs. These are: College of Lake County in Lincolnshire, Illinois; Harold Washington College in Chicago; Normandale Community College in Bloomington, Minnesota; Solano College (virtual) in San Francisco; Houston

Community College in Houston; Montgomery County Community College in Radnor and Fort Washington, Pennsylvania; Community College of Philadelphia; Borough of Manhattan Community College in New York City; and University of the District of Columbia Community College in Washington, DC.

More colleges will likely be added as the program grows; to check the latest listings, go to aon.com/careers/early-careers/us/apprenticeships. And you can check a list of available Aon apprenticeships at jobs.aon.com/jobs.

IBM runs a good-sized apprenticeship program; so does McDonald's, which trains people in management and cybersecurity; at J.P. Morgan Chase, apprentices learn about financial services. Insurance companies, including Zurich, Allstate, and The Hartford, also have adopted the apprenticeship model.

Check with your school, and your school district, on whether it has a professional apprenticeship program. Often, the apprenticeships will be offered only through a limited number of schools in a district, which means you may not find out about it simply by attending your neighborhood school. If your district doesn't have one, you might ask them why not and direct them to CareerWise.

The number and type of apprenticeships is expected to grow quickly and exponentially; there will always be new places to look, so keep searching as time goes on. For that matter, try contacting a company or nonprofit whose work interests you and ask whether they are willing to create an apprenticeship for you. Sell them on your particular interests and skills. Try proposing a specific apprenticeship that outlines the work you could accomplish for them as a trainee, what you'd like to learn by working for them, and how you could best learn it.

In chapter 8, you'll learn about the creative art of baking bread in a wood-fired clay oven, as practiced by a bakery in a scenic area of New Hampshire. The owner of that bakery offers three apprenticeships each year, which includes room and board and a stipend.

On the magically beautiful Orcas Island in Washington State, the Orcas Hotel offers a yearlong innkeeper-chef apprenticeship. "Whether you are looking to become an innkeeper, chef or entrepreneur, this program will be an educational adventure," the hotel's listing said of its 2023 apprenticeship, which provided housing and full-time work paid up to $25 an hour.

A mortuary in Virginia was advertising in 2023 for an apprentice funeral director. It required some training in mortician work, but that's readily available at many community colleges at minimal cost. Even at trainee level, it was paying a salary with full benefits. Some people scoff at funeral homes—until they sadly need a mortuary's help. Morticians' pay ranges up to about $90,000 and more in some places. And because death is inevitable, this is one line of work that isn't going away soon.

The Wolf Trap Foundation for the Performing Arts in Virginia was advertising for a paid costume design apprentice.

Not all jobs listed as apprenticeships actually fit the role, so be cautious. Sometimes, an employer will be looking for some very low-paid temporary help to do work that's only marginally related to what interests you and not really training people for a future in a rewarding job. But overall, expect big increases in the numbers of valid apprenticeships. A general online search, or one on a generic job site, will yield all kinds of intriguing possibilities.

WHITE-COLLAR APPRENTICESHIPS

Where are the white-collar apprenticeships? Here are a few to get you started.

IBM offers full-time, paid apprenticeships under its New Collar program. Its website says, "Our apprenticeship program does not require a bachelor's degree. It is a pathway built for individuals who have acquired some relevant or adjacent skills, but most importantly those who are motivated to learn."[1]

Google also offers many apprenticeships for people of all education

backgrounds. Check out their program and open spots at buildyourfuture
.withgoogle.com/apprenticeships.

The Chicago Apprentice Program includes more than thirty employers, all in the Chicago area. They all are work-study programs held in
conjunction with community colleges. You can find the full current list
at buildyourfuture.withgoogle.com/apprenticeships.

Here are the major companies around the country that founded the
apprenticeship networks in their cities or regions.

Chicago: Aon, Accenture, Zurich

Washington, DC: Aon, Accenture, Amazon Web Services,
Appteon, NT Concepts, Nestlé USA, and SHRM

Philadelphia: Aon, Accenture, Philadelphia Works, Montgomery
College, Community College of Philadelphia, Merck, Chubb

Minnesota: Aon, Accenture, Best Buy, Pohlad, Daugherty, Greater
MSP, ConnextMSP, Cargill, Zurich

Northern California: Accenture, Adobe, Aon, Apprenti, Bay Area
Council (Lead Coordinator), Greater Sacramento Economic
Council, LinkedIn, San Francisco Chamber of Commerce,
TechSF, Twilio

Houston: Accenture, Amazon Web Services, Aon, Dow Chemical,
Texas Mutual Insurance Company, The University of Texas
MD Anderson Cancer Center, Worley

New York City: New York Jobs CEO Council, Aon, Zurich,
Accenture

Southern California: South Bay Workforce Investment Board Inc.

INTERNSHIPS

Internships are more common than apprenticeships. They are shorter
and not as well paid—sometimes, not paid at all. But they can provide
exciting experiences and terrific training. Most internships want people

who have a bachelor's degree or are pursuing one, but not all of them do. And it's not that difficult to find ones that take people who are attending community college. Here's a selection of good ones:

- *Winemaking*: E&J Gallo has several internships designed to teach you about the management of vineyards, the breeding or growing of grapes, production of wine, and other topics around viticulture, all of them located in the Central Valley of California. They require that you be at least twenty-one (it's wine, after all) and in community college, preferably studying agriculture, business, or another field related to viticulture. Pay is $19.25 to $25 an hour. Go to careers.gallo.com and look up internships.

- *Cooking in a national park*: The Glacier Park Collection, a company that provides lodging, tours, and other services to tourists visiting Glacier National Park, runs a paid internship program for people who are planning a future in the culinary arts. Interns rotate through the stations in the kitchen, picking up skills in the various kinds of cooking; learn to follow recipes; and help organize banquets. Pay is $12.50 an hour, but lodging is free and food is discounted. Plus, of course, continual access to one of the most beautiful spots in the country. They're looking for people who are studying in any accredited culinary program. Go to glacierparkcollection-pursuit .icims.com and search for "culinary internship."

- *Marketing*: Eskimo Joe's Promotional Products Group in Stillwater, Oklahoma, hires interns interested in event planning, social media, and marketing campaigns. The internships are paid and part-time, twenty to twenty-five hours a week. There are a lot of marketing internships, but this one looked particularly good for beginners and requires only a high school diploma, though extra consideration is given for those moving on to some kind of postsecondary education. The company also gives the interns discounts on its food and related clothing line. Go to stanclarkcompanies.applytojob.com.

- *Naturalist*: The Minnesota State Parks take on more than two dozen interns to teach the public about the natural resources and environment at various parks around the state, after providing them with training. They give nature talks and staff the visitor center. Some of the parks are looking for naturalists who can teach fishing. This is only for Minnesota residents, and you have to have finished at least one year of studies at an accredited institution after high school. Pay is $15 an hour. Go to mn.dejobs.org and search for "Naturalist Corps Intern."

There are far too many internships to list here, in too many fields. But you can find them by trying out some terms for the things you're interested in doing, and where in the country you're interested in doing them, at juju.com. It's a general jobs site but includes internships; just be sure to include the word "intern" in your search.

CHAPTER 5

ENTREPRENEURS

There's at least one employer who won't care whether you have a bachelor's degree and who knows that you work hard and learn fast: you.

People can become entrepreneurs—own their own businesses, make their own hours, and build their own incomes—based on the ideas and effort they put into their work, pretty much regardless of their formal education or lack of it.

Some, like the Australian woman who has run a travel public-relations business from the yacht where she and her family live and sail the world, do it to create a life of adventure and avoid the doldrums of living in one place most of their lives. Mortgages are not for them.

Others, like the owner of a flavored-ice company that's growing rapidly in Los Angeles, wanted to create something they love and that excites them.

You might have the idea for a business right now. Even in high school, there are so many possibilities. A teenager in the Midwest started mowing lawns, something that has become a successful landscaping business that employs ten people—and I'm willing to bet there are many more like him.

Of course, most of the country is familiar with the billionaire entrepreneurs who never took a bachelor's degree—Bill Gates of Microsoft and Steve Jobs of Apple immediately come to mind. No one cares what your educational background is like if you have the smarts to build a juicy smartphone.

In fact, Freshbooks Research reports that the number of entrepreneurs without a college degree has been increasing rapidly—from 36 percent to 44 percent in just the two years it tracked. And it found that businesses started by people without degrees made just as much money as those whose founders were college grads.

Even the Wharton School at the University of Pennsylvania, one of the top-ranked business schools in the nation, says you don't need a degree to be a successful entrepreneur—and this is a school whose purpose is to educate people at the college and graduate-school level about business. "In most cases, you do not need a specific degree to become an entrepreneur," its website says. "The knowledge you need to successfully run a business can be picked up through real-world work experience."[1]

Perhaps even more interesting, not one of the entrepreneurs I spoke with came from a privileged background. One grew up poor in a small Texas town. The flavored-ice maker was raised in a middle-class family in Philadelphia.

So if you don't need to be rich to start a business, then what does it take?

One of the free online courses offered by the prestigious MIT Sloan School of Management provides some surprising insight about this. According to MIT professor William Aulet, successful entrepreneurs are not typically the most brilliant kids of the classroom. That's partly because they don't much care about pleasing other people, including teachers. Instead, they zero in on what it is *they're* most passionate about—and do great in whatever course they take on that subject. The other courses? They won't put much effort into those.

In fact, they often cut classes they don't care about and are more likely than others to drop out—which nobody is recommending you do. Chances are you'll need that diploma somewhere down the road.

Aulet dashes another myth about entrepreneurs: "Though everyone thinks of entrepreneurs as mavericks who like to go it alone, the ones most likely to succeed work with a team," he said.[2] They will take risks, but only when they've calculated the odds and figured out that they have an advantage. They're patient, looking for long-term rewards.

They have common sense. They know how things work or they do the research to find out. They're disciplined and purposeful.

In my own discussions with dozens of entrepreneurs, I've found other traits that most have in common. They're great at making connections with others and building a network. They find mentors who help train and advise them. For many, every new person they meet is a possible connection.

And they know that the best way to make connections isn't by trying to milk people for all they're worth. Instead, they look for ways to *give* as well as get so that theirs becomes a lasting, mutually beneficial exchange. One of the entrepreneurs you'll meet in this chapter offered to help spread the word about this book when it came out and, during a trip to my area, suggested we meet for coffee. She wasn't asking for favors from me. She just knows that building solid relationships with people and spreading goodwill tends to come back in a positive way.

Finding and building a network takes a little time and effort, but it's not hard to do, even if you're a newbie to the field with no idea of how to start. Facebook might be a messy social media platform that caters to an older demographic, but it's a great place for finding groups of people who share your interest and have more experience and connections than you do. A quick search for "entrepreneur group" on the site brings up a dizzying array of choices, many with thousands of members. The "Women Helping Women Entrepreneurs" group alone has 633,000 members. Even if only 1 percent of those have anything to teach or offer you, that's still more than six thousand potential helpers.

One more thing I found by talking to entrepreneurs: They do not sit on their laurels. They know that when a business isn't going anywhere fresh, it's dying in place. The ones I spoke to all had new ideas hatching. Which also means they're always ready to learn something new. They just aren't choosing to learn it in a typical college course.

Maybe you think that people who own their own businesses are a huge exception in this country, the rare birds who have some kind of secret-sauce knack for making money.

Not at all. According to the US Small Business Administration, 99.9 percent of the companies in this country are small businesses—32.5 million of them.[3]

Depending on which source you consult, it costs around $10,000 to $80,000 in seed money to start a small business. You don't necessarily need a bank loan to get going. According to the Wharton School, there are many groups eager to invest in startups, and crowdfunding sites like Kickstarter have gained real traction as sources of seed money. In 2021, entrepreneurs raised tens of billions of dollars via crowdfunding, according to Small Biz Genius.[4]

All of that sounds inspiring, but how do you actually get started? Every business owner I talked to had his or her unique story. Still, there are a few typical scenarios.

Do you have a hobby or a skill you can exploit? A nephew of mine is an avid fisherman who started out fishing with his grandfather but then practiced and studied up until he became quite the expert. He started a business in high school as a fishing guide, taking other kids to his favorite fishing spots and teaching them the ropes.

Being observant of opportunity is key. Some years ago, a catalog came in the mail selling all kinds of cheap little trinkets in wholesale quantities. Among them were beautiful feathered masks. If you bought a dozen of them, the cost per mask was just $1.25—and shipping was free if you bought *more* than a couple of dozen.

It so happened that some Brazilian friends of mine had just introduced me to Carnival celebrations in my area—events where feathered masks were wildly popular. It wasn't hard to make the link between the two. I bought a bunch of masks; rented booth space at the events; fixed up a table with bright lights, mirrors, and glitzy cloth; and sold the masks for $6 to $12 apiece. It wasn't a living; I already had a full-time job as a journalist. But it was a fun side hustle and brought in significant extra money for working just a few evenings a year.

I could have kept it going—I was starting to sell masks to stores and expanding my sources for finding more elaborate masks—but things were getting too busy in my family and work life to continue. Erin Carey, on the other hand, made a living from her family's way of life.

•

Erin, her husband, and their three sons lived for four years on a yacht, which fit in perfectly with the business Erin has created: doing public relations for the luxury yacht industry.

Erin is originally from New South Wales, Australia; she then moved to South Australia. But until recently, her home and her base of business operations was the sea, very often the Mediterranean. She and her husband did all this without wealth but with absolute determination.

"None of my family had gone to university," said Erin, who's now in her early forties. "No one I ever knew had been to uni. I didn't even know what I wanted to be, and how could I do this four-year commitment and this cost?"

Instead, she went to TAFE, which stands for Technical and Further Education. It provides a flexible menu of programs based on practical skills and apprenticeships that prepare students for employment. It's similar to the community college system in the US but more extensive. There, Erin took a course in retail travel and knew she had found her niche. She'd always loved travel, and her mother had even suggested at one point that she become a travel consultant.

The TAFE course made Erin even more excited about the field. She quickly was hired by the Australian government to book travel for military recruits. "I was getting paid a lot more than any of my friends who went to university and had a secure job right out of TAFE," she said. It was also how she met her husband; he was one of the recruits.

Because he was transferred to Adelaide, Erin moved there too. She got another job in public service and the couple had three sons. Her husband eventually became a public employee as well, and they lived a typical suburban life as middle-income earners, with a mortgage, credit card debt, and family cars.

One night in 2015, her husband turned on a TV documentary about Laura Dekker, the youngest woman to sail around the world. As they watched, they turned to each other and said, "We should do that!"

For most people, the whole idea would have ended soon after as a "someday" fantasy. But Erin and her husband started checking out the blogs of families who were living on boats and traveling the world. "I remember thinking, *If they can do it, so can we.*" They made contact with families who were living the dream, and studied up on everything it would take to live internationally on a boat. That meant taking a sea safety course, reading everything they could get their hands on, and watching countless YouTube videos.

And they started saving. Erin applied for a promotion at work to bring in more money. They canceled insurances and subscriptions and rented out rooms to university students. They borrowed against their home, rented it to Erin's sister, and in 2018 went to pick up their yacht in the Caribbean. They'd taken leave from work; the idea was that this would be just a two-year sabbatical. But they quickly developed a taste for their newfound freedom.

The problem was, they'd saved only enough to get them through the two years. So at the beginning of 2020, they returned to Adelaide to earn more money. Almost as soon as they arrived, the COVID pandemic shut almost everything down. They ended up staying for eighteen months, far longer than they'd planned. Erin got a job she hated in a windowless office. Most important, she found that she and her family were no longer a good fit for their old lives. "We were doing something so much bigger and so much more exciting."

Now they needed to find a way to make money while living on a yacht. "I was wracking my brain," said Erin. "What can I do with the experience I've got?"

During the family's two-year sojourn, Erin had written articles for a number of sailing-related publications, and she noticed that her writing was attracting a lot of attention on social media. That gave her the idea to use those writing skills to open a public-relations agency catering to travel, adventure, and lifestyle companies. A mentor set her up with a course on how to start a PR agency, and during her eighteen months on land in Adelaide, Erin built the business. Today, Roam Generation is not a big agency, but it's busy enough to support the family.

"Most PR people are wearing suits or high heels and don't really know what the sailing life is like," said Erin. "We work with luxury travel companies, and we're able to grow trust among their audience of yachting clients."

Erin and I spoke while their yacht was anchored in Greece. Erin ran the business, and her husband took care of all things boat—mechanical, navigational, and so forth—as well as homeschooling their sons.

Erin is honest about the ups and downs of her family's offbeat life.

"Living on a boat is hard and then sometimes it's just extraordinary fun. You keep getting little bits of amazingness. The lows are really low, but the highs are really high.

"When the toilet blocks, you can't call a plumber. Ducking out to the shop isn't possible. You have to walk to get your groceries. We do have a washing machine, but it's like an eighth the size of a regular machine.

"But we get to travel the world. When we're in a dock, we can just step off the boat and look around. Or we can jump off the boat into crystal-clear water."

More recently, though, the boys wanted to attend high school, so the family has moved back to land for them to complete their schooling. Then, Erin said, she and her husband were planning to head back to sea. "We'll do this until it's no longer fun."

•

Erin's story combines many of the elements that make for successful entrepreneurship. She analyzed her own skill set to determine what kind of business would be a success for her. She prepared like crazy—saved money, took on extra work to bring in more cash, read, found a mentor, networked with others, and formed a team with her husband.

Starting a business requires a lot of new knowledge, not just about your own product or service but about business in general. There are the legal and tax requirements, deciding whether you're opening a corporation or an individual using a fictitious business name. Leadership, creativity, marketing—all this and more goes into opening a business.

In other words, you don't have to attend college to flourish in business, but you *do* have to educate yourself. Probably the best place to start is the US Small Business Administration website (sba.gov), which has materials and courses on practically every aspect of starting a business. The articles are free and responsibly done. Some colleges offer free MOOCs (massive open online courses), such as the minicourses at MIT Sloan School of Management. Online platforms like MasterClass deliver low-cost courses in everything from songwriting to baking to business-specific issues like building a fashion brand. There are countless TED talks, and the list of books on building businesses and entrepreneurship is endless. YouTube has a dizzying number of videos on the subject, but keep in mind that anyone can put up a video. There's no quality control, and it's often there to sell something.

One of the most important steps you can take to avoid heartbreak is the creation of a business plan—even if you plan to crowdfund. Business plans are used to persuade investors to put money into a new venture, but they also show others (and yourself) the forethought you've put into your idea and how (and why) it has a real chance of succeeding. That initial business plan often becomes a blueprint in guiding your first steps in business.

By making a business plan, you vastly increase your chances of success. Let's say you want to open a small gardening or car wash service. What will your durable supplies cost? What will the washing solutions for the cars cost? What will the gas cost to get to people's houses? How will you use social media to get the word out about your business? The Small Business Administration website offers a couple of examples of business plans, one more elaborate than the other.

Even though my mask-selling business involved a minimal investment—about $500 for masks, display equipment, and booth rental, as well as driving to the sites—I still drew up a small informal plan. But I did an entirely different version of a business plan two decades later, when I wanted to leave my newspaper job to start a freelance writing and editing business. My reason for going freelance wasn't to create a winning enterprise. I had been in a coma with encephalitis earlier in the year, and though I emerged in good condition, my doctor said that in order to have a chance of full recovery, I needed to reduce the stress in my life. Daily journalism is a stressful business, and the fact that my newspaper was under constant threat of major layoffs at the time added to the anxiety.

I gathered up all the information about my family's finances to see if I could manage the financial risk. My goal: if I didn't make any money at all, the family still needed to be okay financially until I reached retirement age. We would, I discovered—but just barely, and, like Erin did, we'd have to do some scrimping. That was good enough.

Luckily for me, all of this happened later in my career. Lucky because decades of working in the field meant I already had an extensive network. I started putting out feelers even before I put in my notice to my paper. I was able to work out an arrangement to keep writing for the paper very part-time, as a contractor, at of course a much-reduced income. Friends and former colleagues who were editors reached out to see if I would write for them.

Mentors were still important, though. Again, I was lucky—but in truth, when you go for something you want badly, and you let people know about it, "luck" tends to find you, often in the form of people who want to help and opportunities that might not have caught your eye before. In this case, it was a friend who told me about a secret Facebook group for women writers. It had several subgroups, one devoted just to freelance work, and there I received not just tips about writing gigs but invaluable advice on how to go about the business of freelancing. One of the best pieces of advice got me to change what was starting to be a bad habit: "Don't undersell yourself. Work only for clients who pay well." It was through this group that I found an ongoing client, a health advocacy group in Texas, that became an important weekly paycheck, providing financial stability in this new world.

I also visited a financial consultant who offered an initial meeting for free. He told me how to set up the paperwork for my business and gave me a lot of tax information, including which expenses were tax deductible (using part of my house as business headquarters, for example).

Some important things happened: I found I loved the variety of my new work and the excitement of doing something new. The freedom to arrange my own hours and my own way of working was priceless. I could put in fewer hours and still make more money than I had at my regular job, and it felt reassuring to know that my income depended on my own work and not on uncontrollable factors such as corporate takeovers. I felt the stress fall away and achieved full healing from my illness.

The COVID-19 pandemic was hard on my clients, though, and thus, hard on me. COVID-19 also was the most important story that had occurred in all my years as a journalist, so when my old newspaper offered me a staff job again, I was thrilled to take it. But after a couple of years, I reached the point where it was time to go out on my own again. I've stepped back from a lot of my newspaper work—so of course, I'll be busier than ever.

•

Before you even begin to consider a business plan, ask yourself: *Why will customers flock to my business?* Unless there's a lot of demand for a specific service or product—for example, if there aren't enough landscaping businesses in the area to service everyone who needs it—you'll want to offer something that's at least somewhat different from what people already are getting from existing businesses.

That might mean something like the specialized bakery that recently opened in my town. There's lots of bread on the market, but this business owner is offering an unusual product: organic sourdough breads made the traditional way from sourdough starter, not yeast. She also partners with an organization that promotes the use of heritage grains, which is helping small, local businesses do work that preserves ancient seeds and is good for the environment. Even though the bread is expensive, customers who buy it consider it a special endeavor and feel good about participating. People are willing to pay more for something they see as a superior product that also helps the earth.

My mask business was a product of observation and opportunity. I noticed a number of people at these huge Carnival parties were wearing masks, but none of the event booths were selling them. The masks I'd come across online were extremely pretty and unbelievably low-cost when bought in bulk. (Similar masks, not even as nice, sell singly these days for $35 or so.) By bringing masks to the Carnival parties, I was providing convenience for a reasonable price. It was a small, spur-of-the-moment splurge for people in a partying mood looking for fun, not to save a few dollars.

Erin Carey built her public-relations brand around her intimate knowledge of the yachting world, a life she was living every day. There are plenty of PR companies out there, but few run by a woman who lived on a yacht!

•

Lemeir Mitchell moved to Southern California in 2016 from Philadelphia, where he'd been born and raised. He did it as a leap of faith, to try something different. Little did he know that what he missed about his hometown would launch him into a successful venture as a food entrepreneur.

Lemeir was working as a tattoo artist, a skill he'd picked up through trial and error and YouTube videos. He had no interest in college; he said he had seen the stress it had placed on his mother, a registered nurse, and his brother.

But he was missing something.

Philadelphia water ice, to be exact.

This colorful, sweet treat is very similar to Italian ices and was nowhere to be found in Los Angeles. And that's how Lemeir's business, Happy Ice, was born.

"The reason I started it was that it was something I couldn't live without," he told me.

Lemeir used his savings from his tattoo work to start the company, but he had important mentors, as most entrepreneurs do.

"My uncle Joey was very good friends with someone in Philadelphia who was the leader in the market. My uncle asked if I could intern with him.

"I went back to Philadelphia for about two months and worked for free, learning everything I could, making the product, working with customers and operations. He taught me everything."

When Lemeir's apprenticeship was over, his mentor sold him three months' worth of supplies and the equipment, all for $7,500. The machinery alone was worth about $30,000.

His grandmother helped him buy a food truck, and Lemeir opened for business in September 2017. There wasn't a lot of money for marketing. He and his fiancée gave out free samples outside schools. They set up social media accounts where they posted photos of their first customers, tagging them. The customers would then repost the photos, and word spread.

Eventually, Lemeir bought more trucks and started focusing on the catering end of selling Happy Ice. Why catering? Because sales are guaranteed and paid upfront. All the product can be made in advance, and sales that might take all day in a regular food truck or storefront could be earned in a couple of hours on a catering gig.

Lemeir kept thinking of ways to improve his business. He noted that people in LA were health-conscious, so he reformulated Happy Ice to contain more fruit puree and less sugar. He came up with a scooping method so that a multiple-flavor ball of Happy Ice would have parallel lines of bright colors. He built his own water-ice-making center.

In 2019, Lemeir found an eager investor. He also connected with the head of a chain of restaurants who became a mentor. When I talked to him, Happy Ice was pulling in more than $2.5 million a year, and Lemeir was paying himself a salary of $150,000 and employing thirty people. He's now hired his mom to run a new business: one that will make the Philly cheesesteaks he also misses from his hometown.

Asked to give advice for new young entrepreneurs, Lemeir says that even if you don't go to college or study business in a classroom, "you still have to educate yourself.

"Commit to something—and read," he said. "Ninety-nine percent of the mistakes I made, I read about in a book later. Read the books early so you can move more effectively and make progress quicker."

•

Amber Ybarra is different from most of the entrepreneurs I interviewed. She didn't turn an interest or longtime hobby into a business, or even plan a business based on her background or a goal of making the most money. She's simply tried everything that catches her interest.

Yet the San Antonio woman is also one of the most financially successful businesspeople I've met. She pulls in more than $400,000 a year, and she's only in her midthirties. She's been a model, author, makeup artist, photographer, painter, event planner, and owner of a construction business—often a few of those at the same time.

The way Amber operates, every new experience represents a business possibility. And every person is a potential mentor or at least a member of the network she is constantly building.

It's all a long way from growing up on what she calls the "bad side" of a small town in Texas.

"I had friends who died of drugs and friends who were getting pregnant at fifteen or sixteen," she remembered. "My parents were okay with it if I wanted to stay in my town and have kids at age eighteen."

Amber had much bigger ambitions, however. They began to come to fruition when she was fourteen and singing at town football games and church events. A woman with connections to the modeling world came up to her and said that Amber's height and attractive looks were a good match for modeling. That woman became "a mentor, an angel" who would pick up Amber from school and take her to modeling shows in bigger cities where she found jobs as a curvy, or plus-size, model.

"And that was the life that seemed right for me," Amber said. She wanted out of her hometown as quickly as possible and finished high school within three years, modeling all that time. She signed with an Atlanta modeling agency, traveling in private jets and meeting wealthy and famous people. One celebrity asked for help with her makeup, which got Amber started in that line of work.

Eventually, modeling slowed down and tryouts became too demeaning. "I was too big for straight models and too slim for plus-size," Amber says. "My hips were a half inch too big. Something was always wrong with me."

Then her father got sick. She went home to help her mother and got a menial job at a Subway shop. But she kept her large presence on social media active, and soon a friend connected her with a local who handled city contracts for tourism. Amber's social media savvy and background in fashion shows made her a natural for event production and marketing, and she was hired to put on music festivals, retreats, and other events. She brought in a big new contract for the company and made good money and a lot more connections. Eventually, she felt ready to go out on her own.

Amber's bold and outgoing nature has a lot to do with her success. "I wasn't shy about talking to big names. I would just reach out to people."

When the events world was slow, she would paint six-foot pieces of art and sell them, or do photography to help would-be performers with headshots. She advised performers on how to finesse auditions. She self-published several self-help books that didn't make much money but helped establish her name.

She started dating a man who worked in real estate, fixing and flipping houses. She learned the business from him, and they opened a business together. Although the relationship didn't stick, the business did. Her construction company does privacy fencing, but she keeps up with events, public speaking, and writing.

Amber's advice: Give yourself "permission to fail and permission to try things you enjoy that might not work out." That's how you find out what you want to do—and what you don't.

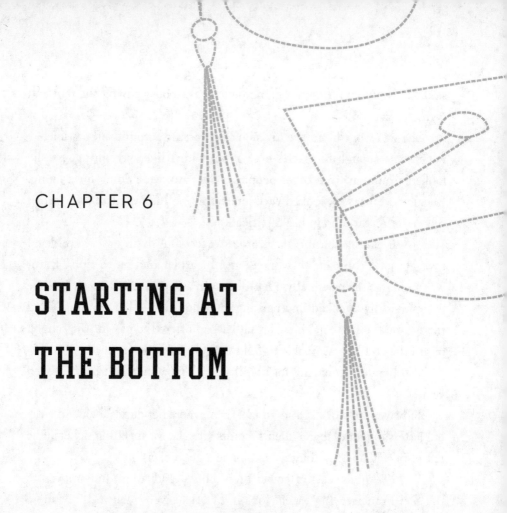

CHAPTER 6

STARTING AT THE BOTTOM

Judy Gielniak had neither the money for college nor the help and guidance of family.

She tried community college but felt aimless. She moved out of her family's Missouri home and worked two jobs, eventually landing a full-time job as a bank teller. But Judy's ambitions far outweighed her early opportunities and resources. She started at the bottom, with jobs that were easy to get without a bachelor's degree, and then proved to employer after employer that she had all the ability of a college grad, and then some.

The quality of her work was noticed right away, and when she applied for a switch to the corporate office in St. Louis a few years later, it was granted swiftly. She wanted to go back to college, but "I didn't have the self-confidence to figure out how I could make college happen," Judy said. "I always regretted not going, but I was so busy paying the rent and trying to live a life."

She was working in the division of corporate accounts on payables—which was enough to teach her that she didn't like accounting. So she looked around at what other people in the bank were doing for a living. Legal assistant work looked very interesting, so Judy went to a for-profit school for a year to gain her certification.

"I was taking that break in order to accomplish an entry-level legal assistant job," she said. "It worked, and I learned a lot on the job." But it was a rough time personally. Her life was in a period of upheaval, and she was physically attacked in a parking lot. She stuck to her training—and then came the financial hit. Her father had offered to pay for the school, but in the end he was unable to follow through on his promise.

"So I ended up paying for it with monthly payments. It took like ten years."

Judy went to work at a small law firm, where her duties included writing letters to judges to get clients' points reduced for speeding tickets. She felt respected and as though she'd made a good decision.

In 1997, nine years after her high school graduation, Judy moved to the San Francisco Bay Area. Jobs in her field were plentiful, but more stressful; legal assistants were treated with less respect, she found. She couldn't find the right employer and found herself job-hopping every eight to fifteen months. She easily found new jobs by working as a temp through legal staffing agencies, so that employers never questioned her patchy employment history. She always did well enough in her temporary jobs to be offered a permanent job within weeks.

There was another advantage to all this career movement—every time she changed jobs, she asked for more money, and got it. She was even recruited for a job as a paralegal, a higher-level job that normally would have required significantly more education, but the firm hired her based on her work experience. Pretty soon, she was making $100,000-plus with overtime.

Judy met and married a lawyer and was able to get a job as a legal assistant at Stanford University, as a member of the clinical education program. She worked with law students on actual cases with clients under heavy supervision. There, for the first time in her professional life, she experienced not just respect for her work but belief in her abilities and intelligence.

"One of my first meetings was an all-hands meeting," Judy said, "and the dean of clinical education was talking about the instruction and how various faculty were teaching. And he said, 'Judy, what do you think is the pedagogical benefit of this?' I came home that day and I remember lying on my bed crying. I had low self-confidence and went through life up to that point not sharing my opinions because I didn't feel they were appreciated, and it was just easier. I had to have an opinion now, and I didn't know what to do with myself."

She and that dean are friends now; he coached her, gave her new opportunities, and when she felt doubtful about taking those chances, "he coached me into spreading my wings."

She was promoted several times at the legal clinic, eventually rising to director of operations of the program. After twelve years there, she took a job at the graduate school of business in a leadership role, but she left in 2019 to try something more daring: starting her own business as a career coach.

She had divorced in the meantime, and both she and her ex-husband moved to Roseville, a town outside Sacramento.

Judy signed up at a training institute and earned her certification as a career coach. She launched her business in 2020—smack in the middle of the pandemic. But by the time we talked in 2022, her business was small but in the black and growing. She was starting to get referrals and did leadership development for a nonprofit educational organization.

In her early fifties, Judy was looking to bring her income into the six figures.

"But I'm not looking to make a ton of money," Judy said. "Lifestyle and helping others are more important to me. I want a balanced lifestyle."

●

Perhaps the most time-honored way of reaching the top without a degree or connections is starting at the bottom in almost any field. The cliché, of course, is the slow-but-steady ascension from mailroom to front office. For some people, it still happens that way. Of course, it also depends on what you call "the top." Finding your way to a fulfilling life with meaningful work might not mean being the biggest boss around.

As Judy's story shows, starting at the bottom can be an especially valuable way to go for people without a bachelor's degree. It gives you a foot in the door and a chance to show how smart, hardworking, and all-around great you are to have in the organization—and how quickly you can learn. For Judy, temporary jobs became permanent jobs. Legal assistant jobs became paralegal jobs. Finally, she was training law students at a prestigious university and being promoted in that setting.

A colleague of mine in journalism who wasn't able to afford a college education started as a copy clerk—in older times, someone who used to carry typed copy to the back shop for typesetting, but who also ran errands including unending trips to the copy machine. Intelligent, involved in the news, and a talented writer, this friend became a reporter and then an editor.

More recently, a New York woman told me about her wife, a lawyer who decided she hated law and went to work for a film company. With all her education, she nonetheless started as a gofer—you know, "go for this, go for that"—and errand worker picking up bagels and coffee for those who ranked above her, which was pretty much everybody else. Now she works in a top creative role at the firm.

Some of the biggest corporate leaders in the United States don't have a college degree. I'm not counting the ones who started their own companies—of course they're in charge of those. I'm talking about the ones who worked their way to the top.

Anna Wintour, the legendary editor of *Vogue* magazine, is among them. She was a fashion rebel at school who got a job as an editorial assistant at a magazine and quickly made her way into editing, with the clear ambition of helming *Vogue* one day. She's known for her ability to build a close network, her extraordinarily long working hours, and her obvious smarts and fashion sense.

Todd Jones, CEO of the Publix supermarket chain, with more than 200,000 employees, started as a grocery bagger with the company.

For that matter, many of the stories you're reading in other chapters of this book involve people who started at the bottom: Mario, who advanced from his volunteer stints with CityYear to running his own nonprofit (chapter 3); Susanna, who took on whatever costume-designing gigs she could find at first (chapter 12); and Jeff, who did tech work part-time for a music store and eventually worked his way into making six figures handling specialized programming for a medical services company (chapter 10).

So how do you go about creating a career this way?

Start by having an idea of what you want to do. My friend knew she wanted to be a journalist. Susanna aimed for Hollywood costume design. Your first job might have little to do with your plans—but the organization you work for definitely should. So do your research. Maybe there's a software company or game design firm whose work you've admired, or a pharmaceutical company coming out with groundbreaking new treatments. Think you need a PhD in biochemistry to do anything major at a company like that? Richard A. Gonzalez, CEO of AbbVie, a global pharmaceutical company, doesn't have a bachelor's degree and earned $26 million in 2022 alone. Of course, he's an exception—but his story also shows that exceptional managerial talent can go a long way.

You want to be around the people *who are doing what you want to do*. That's how you get to observe the work up close, absorb some of it through osmosis, learn through formal or informal training, get a chance to try it, and most important, build a network and quite possibly find a mentor. Remember also that once you're working for a company in the right field, they might help pay for any formal education you need to move on to the next step.

There are plenty of websites about how to work your way up the career ladder. But some of the advice is very obvious, and some of it is archaic. For example, building a network is still one of the most important things you can do in almost any field, but professional mixers aren't how people go about that anymore—for which you should be eternally grateful, because there is no "social" event that feels more forced or phony.

These days, connections are made in more authentic ways: getting to know people in your workplace, in your community, in organizations and clubs around your professional and personal interests, in sports groups, and even at neighborhood hangouts. The size of networks matters less than how close and real those relationships are. Are you and the people in your network just there to use each other, or to help each other and be buddies who care about each other? Do you spend time together without an agenda, or do you contact them only when you want something, though you try to cover that up at first by chatting about other things? Do you get together or just talk vaguely about having lunch sometime soon?

Many of the longtime tried-and-truisms about advancing in your field have become far more complicated in the postpandemic world, largely because of remote work. You can't inhale the atmosphere of a newsroom on deadline from your living room; you can't hang around while people are chatting offline about their best customer strategies. It's hard to offer informally to help out when you can't see coworkers focused on a big project.

Remote work has the great advantages of the flexibility to get things done at home during the workday, wear sweats, build in some exercise, and avoid wasting time in traffic. It's especially great for parents who need to get the kids to school, pick them up, and take them to a play date or soccer practice.

But researchers also have found that remote workers are assigned more work than those in the office, with less recognition for how much they're getting done and lower chances of being promoted. I've also been talking recently with young remote workers at good companies who feel lonely at home. When they go into the office for company, hardly anyone is there—and many younger people find longtime friendships at work. When they apply for transfers to new departments to expand their skills or get a change of pace, it's harder to make the switch because people in those departments don't know them.

A 2022 survey commissioned by Vyopta, a technology services company, found that US executives had some views of remote employees that don't bode well for many people looking to expand their horizons, learn new skills, and work their way up in an organization. And that's especially true of beginners. Substantial numbers of the execs said remote learners were less connected to the company leadership, to colleagues, and to office culture, and that they had less opportunity to collaborate with others. About 95 percent felt that remote workers were less engaged, had fewer opportunities, and were at a disadvantage. More recently, there's been a move by employers to convert remote working positions into outsourced contract positions; they figure that if people aren't in the office, it doesn't matter whether they are fifty miles away or in India.

So even though remote work isn't going away anytime soon, my take is that it's a big mistake for most people who are just beginning their careers right now. Not solely because of problems with raises and promotions and the like, but because it takes most of the exploration, networking, and mentoring out of your life exactly when those are what you most need. You are highly unlikely to come across the unexpected and chat with someone in your organization who's doing something that sparks your interest if you're not there. It's what happens in between accomplishing the formal work that's often most helpful.

There are ways to partially work around it, and some jobs, such as programming, are better suited to remote work than others. There also are employers who work harder at bringing remote employees together. But I'll be frank: Trying to explore the possibilities in a career or a workplace without being there is sort of like trying to figure out what it would be like to become a doctor by taking a biology course. It's a terrific opportunity for people who have had a chance to explore their options, have found their niche, built experience and some reputation. And of course it's near perfect for those who have personal needs at home that make remote work a huge employee benefit.

Despite a couple of cheery lists online of how to overcome the disadvantages of remote working, like checking in with your bosses regularly so they know everything you're achieving, there are few jobs in which you can find and build your career, especially as an employee within an organization, if you are all but disconnected. And Wi-Fi is too thin a thread for the kind of connection you need.

•

Nina Belén Robins didn't have much choice during the pandemic about whether to work remotely or at a physical workplace. As a supermarket employee, she was an essential worker, part of the lifeline that kept people fed during lockdown.

Bipolar disorder made it impossible for Nina to finish high school. Or rather, she said, it was the medications she needed to treat the disorder that kept her from being able to cope with classes.

"I've been in and out of hospitals," she said. "I was living in a residential treatment center. So I went through a program that tries to get people hired."

She started out as a part-time bagger in a local food market outside of New York City at the age of seventeen. Not the most exciting beginning. But Nina would find a community and promotions within her workplace as well as a creative talent outside it.

Nina took her work at the supermarket to heart, and her coworkers and supervisors noticed. She was steadily promoted: full-time cashier, then bakery worker, and now manager of the market's bakery. It's work she enjoys, making sure that the operation runs smoothly and that customers are happy. Sometimes she gets to do the creative work of decorating a cake for a special occasion. And her salary has risen as well; in 2021, she made $65,000. With the salary of her husband, who works in ventilation systems, they're able to live comfortably. She's proud of being debt-free except for their mortgage.

Nina's job is more than a place where her work is appreciated. The supermarket staff formed a protective circle around her. Some of her coworkers can spot signs that she's not feeling well before she's even fully aware of it. When we talked in 2022, Nina, then thirty-eight, told me she'd had a psychotic break the previous winter and her supervisors suggested kindly that her medications weren't working for her and she might need to take a little time off. She got more therapy instead, and a change of medication, and made it through that episode.

She also took a couple of writing classes at the local community college, and her teacher immediately noticed her talent for poetry. The instructor hosted a poetry competition for extra credit, and Nina won it. She began performing at open mic nights for slam poetry, a form of performance poetry, and has performed at bars, libraries, art studios, and even Vassar College. Nina's poetry teacher at the community college is now her friend and hires her to give poetry workshops at the college. She's self-published several books of poetry, including one, *A Bed with My Name on It*, that describes her experience with being institutionalized and the people whose struggles she observed during those times.

One of her goals with her writing is to destigmatize mental illness, she said, and she is honest and open with her readers and listeners. One of her poems, "Pill Bottle," starts out:

> When I think too much
> They take my brain from me.
> Put it in a bottle
> Lock up my thoughts
> With child protective caps,
> Monthly refills,
> And warn me not to operate heavy machinery.
> I give it to them willingly.
> Crawl into sleepy.
> I'm so tired, anyway.

•

Before I started writing at the *Los Angeles Times*, I was an assigning editor there, supervising reporters. Each summer, the paper would hire interns, and one year, one of them was assigned to the edition of the paper that I managed.

She was a bright young woman at a very good local college, but she had no idea what the world of work was like and seemed strangely unable to absorb the rules of the office—such as coming in on time. No one ever made a big deal about someone being ten or fifteen minutes late, or occasionally more. But it was a newspaper, where we responded to news and where there were deadlines for writing it, so wandering in an hour to an hour and a half late, on a regular basis, simply wasn't acceptable. She wanted to write the stories that she wanted to write, which was great. I wanted her to do that too. But sometimes, I needed her to report and write the stories that had to get written.

It feels idiotic to even say this, but for some people it needs to be said: Show up on time (arranged otherwise with a supervisor). Do what needs to be done. Be that dependable person, the one who can always be counted on to be there and get it right. But also talk with your supervisor about the things you'd love to do, the special projects you've dreamed about achieving. It's a rare and very bad manager who doesn't want you to do your best work and love it.

But then, do more. And I'm not talking about working twelve-hour days, day after day, in the thought that this will please some manager who will reward you with the jewels of the organization. My experience is that when managers do notice it, they don't much care and they forget it quickly. They want to show *their* bosses what they have accomplished, not how long their employees have warmed a seat.

I did many of those long stints, excited by the idea that I was necessary to the organization and to the news. Every once in a while, that was true. For the most part, though, I regret the number of numbingly long days I spent in the newsroom as an editor before becoming an opinion writer. That's not the way we should be living our lives. Ongoing stress, lack of exercise, and too little time for community and family are wreaking havoc on our physical and mental health. If, for a while, you're on a project you love that consumes a lot of your time and energy, great. But you don't need to work yourself into the ground to succeed; in fact, it's counterproductive.

Your generation is smarter than mine. I've noticed a lot more emphasis on living a balanced and healthy life rather than working the way up through a narrow path. Employers have noticed it, too, and many of them realize they need to do better than demanding more and more work and hours.

But what does enhance your growth—not just in getting promotions but in finding what you love and crafting a life—is a sense of curiosity, comfort with teamwork, willingness to help others and go beyond the boundaries of the job, plus a never-ending thirst to learn more. When you find out what other people do and let them show you how, you find a mentor and a way to do the kind of work that usually requires a college degree—until you showed that a degree wasn't necessary.

•

Kyle Chambers showed exactly how it can be done.

Kyle was quick in math and science growing up in Southern California, and he scored well on his college-entrance exams, but he hated the tedium of homework. He had good enough grades to get into college; the only problem was that as he was getting his diploma, the Great Recession had hit, his father had lost his job, and his mother was struggling to support the family on $75,000 a year. Despite how tight things were, colleges told him his family's income was too high for him to get financial aid.

He tried community college, but he often felt that he was learning things he already knew. The homework was no more engaging than it had been in high school. "I hated college," he said.

Instead, Kyle served four years in the US Marine Corps reserves, one weekend a month and a couple of weeks each summer as a gunner, while working during the week as a banquet server, then a security guard. He got a foot in the door at Princess Cruises, working various jobs, some successfully and some less so. He was making a lackluster $37,000 a year.

The big break—and the big change in Kyle—came when he was among seven or so employees chosen to beta-test a new customer-compensation system. "I challenged myself to say, 'If I were just coming into this without the training on the system, how would I try to break it?' That was how the company could find the weaknesses in the program and fix them. I was the only one who came back saying, 'Here are the issues, here are the holes you need to fix,' and I really impressed the IT guys.

"And that ended up being a great thing for me because it really launched my career."

It's that crucial step of not just sitting there, nicely doing the basic job, but going for something more—and, in the process, getting noticed.

A revenue analyst in another department was taking several months off, leaving a temporary opening for someone to examine a system that would automatically price cruises for specific areas at specific times. The IT staff recommended Kyle for the job. His salary, as long as the temp role lasted, would go up to $52,000 a year.

"I told myself that I was going to make myself so invaluable to that team that they wouldn't want to get rid of me. I became so instrumental that even though the team for domestic cruises couldn't keep me, they opened a role for me working on international cruises."

An important note about this new job: it had previously required a bachelor's degree. Kyle proved that not only was a degree unnecessary, but that the best candidate for a job might end up being the guy without one.

How did he do it?

The project was using Excel software. Kyle learned everything about it he could, watching YouTube videos in the evenings after work.

"I automated a lot of the use of Excel," he said. "I would speak up in meetings when I disagreed or when I saw a different pattern that could be used. I made everyone's workday a little easier by making all the pricing sheets and promotional sheets automated.

"That was how I became instrumental."

Working on the international cruises involved another platform, Tableau, that Kyle said could be coded to provide more refined data. He dug into the platform's free tutorials after work to master the system. "I automated all the reports we had so that it would update automatically."

Kyle wasn't just going beyond the basics in his job; he was putting major effort into learning more.

The manager of marketing and analytics, a woman highly respected in her field, was offering classes during lunch one day a week, and Kyle signed up.

"I loved it. I loved what she was throwing down." He told her he'd like to be considered for any openings on her team. She'd noticed how engaged he was, and when an opening came up six months later, he got it—a job, once again, listed for college graduates only.

Kyle hadn't just earned a new job and a nice bump in pay, to $68,000. He'd found a mentor. "She was the first boss I had who went out of her way to highlight her team's achievements, not her achievements." Kyle worked on analyzing past marketing efforts so that the company could better target customers based on their attributes, such as whether they had gone on cruises before. He learned from his teammates and was promoted to a senior role, making $93,000.

And when the pandemic struck and cruise trips came to a halt, almost the entire team was furloughed for six months, but Kyle and the manager were still working full-time, albeit at reduced salaries.

The department was restored after the furlough. Then Kyle's boss left and recommended that he be made manager of the department. But the company wouldn't do it.

Remote work had become the new thing. Kyle moved to the Fort Worth area of Texas to be near a close friend; he was still working for Princess, but his excitement about the company was fading. He updated his LinkedIn profile, was contacted by a recruiter, and went to work for a company that makes filters, at $125,000 a year, as a digital solutions lead. But he hadn't known the marketing team was going through some dramatic changes, and he stayed only a year. He saw a firearms manufacturer doing what he considered to be some brilliant marketing moves and thought, *I can really learn from those people.* So he applied to work for them remotely and now, in his early thirties, finds it a good fit with welcoming people, even though he works for $10,000 less as a senior business-intelligence analyst.

His advice: Make sure the people you're working with are warm and welcoming. Be sure to create an excellent résumé—hire pros if you need to—and keep a strong, updated LinkedIn profile.

Never underestimate your own abilities. Keep learning, learning, learning.

And above all, never be afraid to ask—for a job or promotion, for information, or for training and resources.

•

Robert Parker faced a different set of obstacles, but like Kyle, he doesn't give up easily.

As Robert was growing up in Virginia and then New Jersey, his mother noticed that he avoided eye contact and that his speech seemed delayed. "There was something different about me," he said. "Like they'd say my name and I wouldn't respond." When he was two years old, his mother took him to the doctor to try to figure what was going on.

He was sent to a school for children with developmental delays, where he received extra time and help. And he had a good experience there, both academically and socially.

But having friends and schoolmates with various kinds of learning disabilities, Robert came to wonder what he had, so he asked his mother outright.

"You have autism," she told him, "but you're higher functioning."

Robert wanted to go to college, but a job coach at his high school tried to talk him out of that. She didn't take into account just how determined he was to learn things that didn't come easily to him.

He attended community college despite what the job coach said, taking three years to earn his associate's degree in TV production. He got involved in drama and worked with the theater's sound system.

But finding a full-time job with benefits was tough. He applied for a part-time job in TV production but was turned down. So he went to work at Target for a couple of years, starting out by stocking shelves part-time, making minimum wage and a meager $7,000 or so a year. The pay was bad, but the job felt even worse to him.

"They liked that I was very determined and came to work ready to go," he said. "They made me a cashier. I really liked that because it was dealing with people face-to-face, getting out of my comfort zone."

He left after a couple of years but remembers the company fondly. "It was the first company that gave me a chance," Robert said.

An uncle of his with ties to the Society for Human Resource Management suggested he try applying there. The Virginia-based organization is a professional association for human resources officers—and promotes the idea that not everyone should need to go to college to get a good job.

When we talked, Robert's work situation was at a whole new level. In his midtwenties, he works full-time as a facilities specialist, making $48,000 a year plus benefits. His job requires independence and responsibility; he makes sure every room, every machine, is equipped as it should be and working properly. He sets up the rooms for events and keeps things running smoothly. He feels respected and in a stable situation.

Even better, he started talking to people higher up at SHRM about doing video production for their conferences and other events, and they've been encouraging. It would give him experience in the work he's been wanting to do for years.

"Don't be afraid to take a chance on yourself," he advises those who are starting out. "People tried to put me in a box. I kept asking questions and just kept going."

TEN TIPS FOR STARTING AT THE BOTTOM—AND NOT STAYING THERE LONG

The following behaviors may not launch you to the top, but on the other hand, not doing them pretty much guarantees that you won't get anywhere fast—or at all.

1. *Do the basics.* Show up on time. Work a full day, at least on average. Don't skim through the day just because you can. Let your supervisor know what you're doing. Work carefully; don't just get it done, get it done right. And meet deadlines.

2. *Make it special.* Look for ways to make your projects stand out. Don't add new elements just for the sake of adding them, but think about ways you can organize the work or provide needed information that take it beyond the ordinary. That's especially true when you're responding to the requests of a boss; show you really listened and try to give supervisors even more of exactly what they want.

3. *Lend a hand.* Offer to help others, even if you get no credit. You'll learn about new aspects of the job, build your teamwork skills, and begin building a network.

4. *Maintain a record.* Supervisors have short memories. Keep written track of the best work you do, when you did it, and what made it special. Come performance-evaluation time, there's a good chance you'll be given a chance to do a self-evaluation. Don't blow that off; it's a valuable opportunity. Make an impression with the reminders of the outstanding work you did. I once had a boss I didn't particularly like or get along with, and in her evaluation of me, she basically picked up my self-evaluation almost word for word and gave me a big raise—and in the process changed her attitude toward me.

5. *Work hard.* Don't be the kind of person who jumps up and leaves exactly at quitting time as though there were an ejector spring in your chair. It gives the impression that you are not engaged

enough in your job to spend an extra few minutes. At the same time, do not put in sixty-hour weeks. For one thing, you'll be less productive, strange as that might seem, and you'll burn out faster. And no one will really notice or remember. Work fiercely during work hours, but respect your life and your body enough not to become a workaholic. If you're in a workplace that will hold you back because you don't give them your whole life, find another organization. Those people are bound to find something to be unhappy about anyway.

6. *Set a goal.* Make it specific, and let others know what it is. Even if you decide to change the goal later, it's helpful to work with a purpose in mind. And if your boss or colleagues know what your goal is, chances are they'll let you know about work opportunities or trainings that align with what you want.

7. *Dig in and show up.* Get to know people throughout your department and in other departments as well. Learn how things work. You never know what tidbit will open a new world to you, what new interest you might develop, or what new openings are coming up that might interest you.

8. *Ask questions.* There is no such thing as a dumb question. Well, yes, there is, but rarely, and it's a lot better to ask than remain ignorant. People like being expert enough to answer questions, and they love talking about what they do. So ask. Show interest. Just be careful not to pester.

9. *Ask about further learning opportunities.* Find out what training your employer offers, what outside education it might pay for completely or in part, and what kind of training has been most helpful to other employees, both supervisors and coworkers. They'll appreciate your desire to continue to learn in the job. There's nothing wrong with asking, "How can I learn to do that?" Don't forget to learn what you can on your own, using YouTube tutorials and the like. Decide to be the expert on whatever your team or company is doing. It will show.

10. *Start out in person.* Try to start your career at an in-person business so that you can more easily meet people, build relationships, and see up close how things operate. Supervisors are more likely to see and appreciate the work you do as well. At least try for a hybrid place where most workers come in a few times a week; there's little point in going to an office where no one but you is there. Once you're more established, remote is fine, as long as you go out of your way to communicate with your coworkers and supervisors and are clear about what you've been getting done.

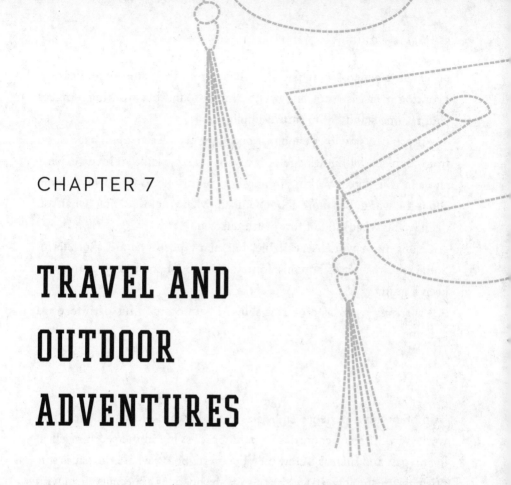

CHAPTER 7

TRAVEL AND OUTDOOR ADVENTURES

This is the chapter for adventurers: those who crave travel and outdoor experiences—which often overlap.

There's hardly a better time in your life to travel than right now. It's fun and fascinating and a lot more. Spending real time overseas—not just a couple of weeks looking at museums and countryside but as a resident getting to know the people and way of life—gives you a great start on your future life. In this global economy, it's worthwhile to understand how other cultures operate while making international contacts; you never know when a new friend will turn into the gateway to a career. Working overseas—not just backpacking around but working—makes your résumé stand out to future employers.

If you can stay long enough, you might even learn a language or go from high school knowledge of it to full fluency. Like so many experiences in this book, working in another country not only tells you more about the world, but more about yourself, what you love doing, what you dislike, and what kind of future attracts you.

Long-term work is available, but many positions are short-term. Some require a bit of hopping from job to job, or country to country, to keep it going.

Working overseas on farms showed Sam Stanton his path forward at home.

•

Sam Stanton's experience embodies the full range of this chapter. Sam worked in different countries in outdoor jobs. He immersed himself in boat repair and then as a crew member on tugboats, where the pay is surprisingly great. Now, at age thirty-nine, he operates a specialty farm with his wife on an island at the northern edge of Puget Sound in Washington State.

Sam's path wasn't linear; it involved a lot of exploration, learning, and willingness to try new things. Originally from Portland, Oregon, Sam dropped out of high school but then completed it. He attended college for three years before deciding it wasn't heading him in the direction he wanted. He later completed college, but not before having adventures, establishing himself in a lucrative trade, and finally becoming an agricultural entrepreneur.

One of his big interests was in sailing tall ships and training vessels. "I got excited about boats and wanted to play on shipyards," he said. So, after dropping out of college, he attended trade school for a year, learning boat repair, and had some internships in the maritime industry.

There's plenty of work in the boatyards and shipyards of the Northwest. In fact, Sam said, demand is so high that he probably didn't need the trade school education, though it gave him an edge.

"They would have hired me if I'd just gone down to the boatyard," he said. "Tall ships pay pennies, but they'll hire anyone with a pulse."

Then Sam transitioned to tugboats, "moving oil barges around." Tugboats are federally regulated and require a drug test—and there's a shortage of people who can pass the test, Sam said.

Crewing on tugboats isn't exactly a nine-to-five job. The crew member lives on the boat and might need to travel anywhere in the country. The work is one month on, one month off, though people can take more time off if they want. The pay is a big attraction. Sam made $125,000 in a year by learning the mechanics of the engineering room over time. But remember, that's working just six months of the year. Anyone who fills in the "off" months with other work can make a lot more. Or they can use the money to fund themselves while they work on unpaid or low-paid projects that are their passion. Or . . . they can run a farm.

Sam isn't one for doing the same thing all the time. Those years also took him on some short-term gigs working overseas. In his case, he used New Zealand's working holiday visa to take several jobs there.

In 2023, six countries had working holiday visa programs that accept American citizens: Australia, Canada, Ireland, New Zealand, Singapore, and South Korea. These programs are geared to people like you: ages eighteen to thirty. Unlike regular work visas, they're easy to get—you mainly just need to show some form of financial stability, and you don't have to nail down a job before going there.

But the programs come with restrictions: the work is mostly part-time, since it's supposed to include study time, and is mainly limited to jobs such as childcare, hotel staff, fitness instructors, restaurant or bar servers, tour guides, or other jobs that revolve around the tourism industry. In New Zealand and Australia, however, many of the jobs involve farming or ranching.

Sam did some hotel work but then found his way to a couple of farms via the nonprofit known as WWOOF (World Wide Opportunities on Organic Farms). WWOOFers, as the workers are known, work on farms in exchange for room and board. These kinds of arrangements have become a major way for young people to travel all over the world for essentially the cost of getting from one place to another, as well as learn the practicalities of farming. The gigs have their upsides and their problems, which we'll get into later in this chapter.

Like many WWOOFers, Sam had great experiences and bad. His first New Zealand farm was a good one; his six weeks there formed the direction for his life. "It was a permaculture project demonstration farm," he said. "It got me very excited about being outside and taking on a project like that on my own. It was a fairly new farm, just getting started, so I just had a blast with it."

The work included construction, starting seeds, animal care, beekeeping, and farming a vegetable garden. That was perfect for Sam.

"I'm someone who really likes a diversity of tasks," he said. "If I'm doing the same thing every day, I'm not happy."

Sam also got a paid job as a hotel porter as well as a paid farm stint that he hated, picking tangerines. Workers were paid by the tree, so the slower workers made out badly and were eventually fired, and the faster workers would get transferred to bigger trees, so they didn't do well either. Then he got a paid job as a sailing instructor, which he found fun and rewarding. It also paid enough for him to get by.

How did he find these jobs? He started with WWOOF, as many do, and from there began reaching out to others.

A completely separate gig in Malaysia through a program called Help Exchange went bad, though. "It was a farm that wasn't doing very well," he says. "It was kind of falling apart, and they were losing the battle with the jungle. They didn't have the skill set or enough energy." Still, the international experience was worth it. "I'd wake up early in the morning to the sound of gibbons howling, and the farmers would sleep in until 10 a.m. It was an absolutely beautiful place."

Back in the United States, Sam decided to complete his degree.

He arranged with a professor of marine studies at the Evergreen State College to get the credits for his senior year by working on an ocean research vessel for several months and keeping a careful journal of the experience. It's the kind of thing you can't do at many four-year schools. (Learn more about Evergreen, an exceptional public college where you can design your own studies and receive credit for work experience, in chapter 12.)

Sam's wife, Caitlin, also worked in the maritime industry, on tugboats on the Columbia River, and is a grant writer. Farming was a dream the two had in common.

"It was something we talked about almost since the day we met."

The couple spent about two years searching for property. In 2016, they found a twenty-acre parcel, a long-abandoned homestead, on Whidbey Island about thirty miles north of Seattle. They went in with friends, each taking ten acres, and were able to come up with the funding. The purchase included a house in need of a lot of repairs; they lived in a trailer on the land while the work was underway.

Their farm, Whidbey Herbal, makes essential oils from lavender grown on the farm and from tree branches knocked down by the wind.

"I'd learned to do some natural product extraction at school," Sam said. "I focused on chemistry at Evergreen."

As an agricultural product, aromatic oils are a practical way to get started. They have a long harvest window and a long shelf life; there's little need for continual field work or a sudden, overwhelming harvest. "I needed to grow things that could handle my going away" on tugboat runs, to earn the money to keep things solvent, Sam said. The farm also runs a mushroom operation but doesn't advertise it because there's no need; the mushrooms all sell out at the farmer's market.

The farm's red ink turned to black at the beginning of 2022, though Sam is keeping his options open by renewing his tugboat license. He'd rather not go back to the boats at this point, though; he and his wife have two young children.

Sam's a big believer in the notion that college isn't for everyone, even though both his mother and grandfather have doctorates. He sees science as one of the few fields that call for a formal higher education.

"College is kind of an outdated way to learn things. There's so much you can learn through life experience. You can get direct access to people; you can go participate in things." In his view, many people go to college more to party and try to find a partner rather than be educated for their future lives.

He wouldn't put his degree on an application for tugboat jobs. "They don't want a 'college boy.' They want someone to do the job."

•

Farming and overseas work are natural companions these days, but be aware that most of the jobs are volunteer and short-term and compensate you only with room and board. It is pretty easy, though, to find longer-term stays or line up one stay after another for a variety of experiences.

In truth, though websites love to use the word "volunteer," I don't think of these jobs as volunteer work. Though some of the organizations involved are nonprofits, most are not. They're farms or hostels or other businesses, though they might be businesses engaged in doing good things for people and the world.

It's more or less a work exchange. You give about five hours a day of work, are free to enjoy your life in a foreign setting the rest of the time, and are given room and board in exchange for your labor. That doesn't make it a bad thing; it's just helpful to be aware of the real agreement. One listing I saw was to be a maid and cook for a wealthy family who live in a lovely coastal home and are too cheap to pay someone for a hard day's work. That might be fun, but there's a limit to how great you'll feel being an unpaid servant for rich people who won't pay a decent wage, and cleaning houses is unlikely to lead to new skills or connections with different kinds of people. It won't help you discover yourself and the world.

There are three particularly popular websites for finding overseas gigs: WWOOF, Workaway, and Worldpackers. Where WWOOF is devoted solely to farm jobs, Workaway and Worldpackers list all sorts of jobs and have more variety. So if you know that organic farming is what you want to do and learn about, and you know one or a couple of countries that interest you, WWOOF might be a better fit. (In addition to having had a great experience WWOOFing, Sam Stanton has brought WWOOFers to his farm to work.) Otherwise, you're probably better off with Workaway or Worldpackers, where you can find jobs as a hostel worker, tutor, tour guide, and the like.

WWOOF is decentralized, with different organizations and websites for the various countries involved. That also means there's a separate fee for each country, though there has been talk of putting all the listings into one centralized place. On Workaway and Worldpackers, you can find all the world's listings on one website, for one price. Accessing the work database for either costs somewhere in the $60 range.

With all of these sites, you pay for your own travel to the workplace and work about five hours a day. For WWOOF, that's six days a week; with Workaway, it's five. Worldpackers sets a limit of thirty-two hours a week but recommends that hosts ask for only twenty-five hours a week, with two days off.

There are caveats in taking these jobs, especially jobs in remote areas where farms are more likely to be located. In addition to the many good experiences WWOOFers have had, many complain about bad ones. These include dirty sleeping arrangements; doing scut work like the housework and laundry instead of farm work (and the farm work itself is often physically taxing); and being told to do more hours and days of work than you're supposed to. Sam Stanton said he's heard from some of the WWOOFers he's hired about being required to work sixty hours a week at some farms. The websites include reviews of the various hosts, and those might or might not be fully accurate. Certainly, any place with several negative reviews is somewhere you probably don't want to go.

A surprising number of WWOOFers also complain about being provided with an inadequate amount of food, especially considering that they often are engaged in hard physical labor.

The advice from experienced veterans of all the groups: Communicate, communicate, communicate before taking a gig. Make clear what your boundaries are: that you work no more than a certain number of hours a day and a certain number of days. Ask what the food is like and the amounts. Will you eat with the family or be given rations to prepare on your own? Request photos and descriptions of the living conditions. It's rare that hosts will out-and-out try to scam you; most of the problems come from lack of clear understanding on both sides.

It's also a good idea to determine the location of the nearest town and what transportation is available. Think twice about going somewhere you'll feel stuck.

Alumni of WWOOF and Workaway suggest arranging a backup gig if the one you're starting turns sour, but I'd be cautious with that. It's unfair to lead a host to think you'll be there if they're just an escape route, so be upfront with them about it. More important: make sure you have the money and means to leave if it comes to that. Some work exchangers prefer Worldpackers for this reason; its insurance program gives you a place to stay for a week if the host has made it impossible for you to feel comfortable staying.

•

Taylor Herperger turned her Worldpackers experiences into a career as a travel writer.

Originally from Saskatchewan, Canada, Taylor tried university after high school but said it "didn't click" with her. She then went to a private two-year school to study the music business.

She worked at Warner Music for a few years as a promotions coordinator, but also wrote a travel blog on the side during her lunch hours. "I've always loved writing," she said.

At age twenty-five, she quit her job and gave in to her yearning to see the world, finding her first gig at a hostel in Spain through Worldpackers, interacting with guests, getting things ready for the day, giving guided tours, and doing limited cooking.

She worked three to four days a week and was free to explore the rest of the time. In exchange, she received dorm-style accommodations and food and was paid under the table. Some hostels will more openly give workers a stipend. Taylor found that Worldpackers' reviews from people who had worked at hostels before were solid and that the organization did a particularly good job of getting newbies fully ready for their experience.

From there, Taylor worked her way through hostels for five months and has now been to nineteen countries, mostly in Europe but also Mexico and Central America. Once home, she was able to parlay her travel expertise into writing a column for an offbeat lifestyle magazine, which led to her being hired as an editor (while she kept writing) at Travel Lemming, an online travel guide, making about $50,000 a year. Two months after I interviewed her, she was promoted to director of marketing and senior editor for the site. Now in her early thirties and living in Winnipeg, Canada, she has managed to combine her two great loves, travel and writing, into a thriving career.

There are other "voluntouring" sites, but in general, beware of the ones in specialized fields that sound especially compelling, such as those in animal refuges. Usually, these involve paying a hefty sum for the privilege of putting in hours of work every day. That's not volunteering, and it's not living amid a new culture and learning to make your way; instead, you're simply a paying tourist.

There is an organization that will take volunteers for a year or more; it's covered in chapter 3 on volunteering. Camphill, a collection of "intentional communities" for developmentally disabled adults that do biodynamic farming and a wide range of trade skills including baking, woodworking, and bottling herbal supplements, has twenty-two locations outside the United States, most of them in Europe. The nonprofit organization provides room and board and a living stipend.

●

It's not as easy to make a living overseas as it was a couple of decades ago, especially if you've got your heart set on being in Europe. Work visas there are very hard to obtain because of laws that require first consideration of EU citizens. Few employers are willing to go to bat for someone from outside the EU, and that applicant needs to have some kind of outstanding skills; this is one place where college grads have an edge, though it's extremely difficult for them as well.

That said, there's also a new way for people to live and work long-term in Europe and on just about any other continent, as long as they don't work for an employer in that country. Just over the past few years, many countries have created "digital nomad visas." In other words, if you have an employer from outside the EU who allows you to work remotely, these countries will allow you to live there. It also works for people who are self-employed or freelancers. This is a great option for computer programmers or other people who can land US jobs that allow fully remote work. Just be prepared to work some strange hours because of the time difference.

At least forty countries offer digital nomad visas, including Thailand, the Bahamas, Belize, Brazil, Portugal, Norway and Malta (where English is one of the official languages), Greece, and Seychelles. The programs are catching on rapidly; several other nations are working on offering them, so check online for the latest.

Most of the visas require proof of income. For some countries, that means a specific amount per month. Other countries just require sufficient income to live there. You'll need your own health insurance and a record clean of any crimes. The length of the visas ranges from six months to a couple of years, but most are renewable.

Another way to gain entry for work in another country is by teaching English as a foreign language. Yes, usually this requires a bachelor's degree—but not always. Among the countries that *don't* require one are Argentina, Brazil, Cambodia, Chile, Costa Rica, Curacao, Mexico, Nepal, Peru, and Romania. What they will require is a TEFL (Teaching English as a Foreign Language) certificate, after you take a course that ensures you understand the rules of English usage and instructs you in teaching a language. Those courses are available at prices ranging from about $90 to $1,600, online and in person; the important thing in becoming a competitive candidate is to select a course that requires at least 100 hours of study, and even better, 120 hours. The courses usually take a few months of online study and testing.

Anthony DeGeorge took a different route to spending time overseas. He started with a short-term stint at culinary school that he was able to parlay into spending two years in Italy and then building a successful career as a chef. His career has included a tour in Japan and Australia with Cirque du Soleil, jobs in several kinds of restaurants, his own business cooking and delivering meals during the pandemic, a nonprofit for kids, and most recently working as a chef for special events at the iconic Country Music Hall of Fame and Museum in Nashville, Tennessee.

Anthony was born to the restaurant business; his restaurant-manager mother got him his first job busing tables when he was a teenager. He liked the work, and, strange to say, he liked working in restaurants even more if he was called on to wash dishes when someone called in sick. The informal camaraderie in the kitchen felt fun and offered a path to advancement. Any downtime a kitchen worker has can be used to start helping out in the kitchen, starting with vegetable preparation, then salads and onward. He found that he was naturally talented at it.

"It's nice to be good at something and especially at that age to have people that you look up to constantly shower you with praise because you're really good at cleaning mushrooms or whatever."

Usually, training to be a chef entails attending culinary school, which is shorter and less expensive than college, but often takes a year to two years to complete at a cost of from $20,000 to $40,000. Many community colleges offer culinary arts certificates and degrees for a fraction of the money.

But as Anthony worked in various restaurants and talked to the people there, he said, "Everyone told me, 'Don't waste your time, don't waste your money [on culinary school]. They're going to take a huge amount of money from you and teach you stuff you could be paid to learn on the job.'"

Anthony was able to work his way up in many kitchens but eventually decided that an experience cooking internationally might be a help. He was particularly interested in the Piedmont area of Italy, where the cuisine has its own distinctive dishes and style. He applied for a job at an Italian restaurant, and the interview was going nowhere until he mentioned his interest in Piedmont. It turns out the restaurateur had gone to a culinary institute there. At that point, the conversation turned, and Anthony was hired. He worked at the restaurant for about a year, saving up money to attend a course at the Italian Culinary Institute for Foreigners in Piedmont.

The courses are specialized, geared toward giving professionals the techniques and knowledge of the area's cooking, and the Institute provides internships at nearby restaurants while students live in dormitory-style housing. It costs several thousand dollars, but much less than the usual US culinary schools. The most important part, Anthony knew, was what he would learn in the kitchens of the region's restaurants—and he did, at an eatery where he said the staff were talented and paid great attention to detail.

Anthony was working hard and accomplishing a lot in the kitchen. But he ran out of money and went to the head chef asking for a job. Without a work visa, he couldn't get a regular job, but the chef offered to pay him under the table, which was how he stayed in the country for two years. While doing that, he also worked some shifts at other restaurants, learning everything he could and loving the experience of working with others from all over the world (he wasn't the only foreign intern).

The experience helped open doors for Anthony back in the United States. He got a job as head chef in a small Italian bistro. The owner's mother didn't speak English, so his newly acquired Italian language skills came in handy as well.

Later on, a one-week gig helping out with the cooking for Cirque du Soleil in Portland turned into a longer-term job touring with the celebrated circus troupe in Japan, Taiwan, and Australia. The cast was so diverse that it gave him another chance to work with people from all over the world and cook different kinds of cuisines.

Returning to Portland, Anthony became a sous-chef at a restaurant for plant-based food, and then was promoted to executive chef. He then moved to Nashville, Tennessee, to be executive chef at another plant-based restaurant. It closed during the pandemic, so Anthony started his own business cooking and delivering meals and organized a nonprofit offering cooking classes for kids.

But then came the opportunity to work for the Country Music Hall of Fame and Museum. In addition to its music and education missions, the Nashville entity runs a banquet program in its elaborate event hall that Anthony says generates $17 million a year.

Now, at age forty-one, Anthony earns more than $90,000 a year. He highly recommends an overseas experience, or at least immersion in somewhere away from home, not just for cooks but for everyone.

"Regardless of what you want to do with your life," he said, "everybody should leave the town they grew up in and go to where people are completely different from what they're used to. Learn someone else's culture and surround yourself with a diverse group of people. It's important for us to do that to grow."

•

Of course, you don't need to travel overseas to work on a farm or do most kinds of outdoor work. As Sam Stanton showed, it's not difficult to get jobs working in boatyards. You can WWOOF right here in the United States and find a certain amount of variety. One listed gig puts you on a working dude ranch and bison reserve in Montana; former WWOOFers rave about the experience.

Aside from short-term jobs, the opportunities for outdoor work without a degree are practically limitless. Landscapers and gardeners are in heavy demand. Arborists (tree specialists) generally earn more. Dog trainers bring in good money. If you know animals or, even better, how to work with heavy machinery, it's not difficult to get a job as a ranch hand. Construction has long been the kind of work that draws outdoors-oriented people. Firefighting and law enforcement are also traditional paths.

But the possibilities go far beyond the obvious, especially if you are willing to start at the technician or assistant level. Just as Anthony said about the restaurant business, a lot of fields are better learned by doing rather than by getting a degree. It's also how many people learn whether a certain field appeals to them, which might ultimately lead them to seek whatever education is needed to move up the ladder. (See the box of possibilities in this chapter.)

Most park rangers these days hold bachelor's degrees, for example, but it's often not a requirement. A lot depends on the agency involved. The National Park Service doesn't require a degree, but for those who don't have one, it's not the place to start looking because of the many requirements around experience. A better place to start your search might be state or local parks.

Saying "local parks" may sound silly. What, overseeing the wild children at the playground? Hardly. The county where I live, though very small geographically, runs many wilderness parks and reserves. Becoming a ranger here involves getting a diploma or equivalency degree and successfully completing the county's Ranger Academy.

Recruits attend free, taking sixteen weeks of courses plus six additional weeks of field training. The Academy provides all the equipment needed and teaches everything from law enforcement to wilderness first aid. Many of the recruits come from the county's ranger reserves, a volunteer program that involves working at least eighteen hours a month in the parks, but that's not necessary to become a ranger.

And there are other parks jobs, such as maintenance or park attendant, that don't require any degree or an academy, but that allow you to live and work outdoors in beautiful natural places.

Remember, as you apply for jobs at the technician or assistant level, that even if most of the jobs say that a degree is preferred, employers are having a tough time filling positions these days. Take advantage of it and put yourself out there. There are people who won't apply for a job if they see they're lacking maybe 20 percent of what an employer wants; be aware that those lists of qualifications are generally wish lists, not set-in-stone requirements. Other people will apply if they have 20 percent of the qualifications for a job. Be one of those people and accentuate the qualifications you do have, including ones they might not have considered.

You also greatly enhance your chances if you can start in a field where you already know a thing or two, regardless of whether that's from formal training or just from having engaged in an activity you love.

Brandon Ware spent much of his childhood fishing with his father, who had fished with his father. On that side of his family, Brandon is descended from the Tlingit, the Indigenous people of southeastern Alaska. He has lived all his life, except for a short stint at college in Washington State, in the small island town of Petersburg, adjacent to the massive Tongass National Forest.

Brandon said he grew up "walking in two worlds," the term that Indigenous people use to describe balancing the traditional life of their groups and the larger Western world. Brandon was raised Catholic and attended regular public schools, but he also was steeped in Tlingit culture, including reverence for elders and a sense of stewardship for the land and water, for the salmon and halibut that traditionally make up the majority of his people's diet. Brandon is his Western name; his Tlingit name is ShaaL'aanee, which Brandon said means Fish Trap.

It's the perfect name, as it turns out, because Brandon, at age twenty-three, earns his living several months a year running a fishing guide business, using his deep-water boat to catch salmon, halibut, and other ocean fish, and a flatboat for river fishing.

Though it seems like a natural fit, Brandon wasn't sure what he wanted to pursue after high school. He started out with a course at a local college that earned him his captain's license. Around that time, he took a friend out on his boat for a fishing derby. After the friend caught a couple of large salmon and halibut, he told Brandon, "You really ought to look into doing this as a job."

The idea clicked. But first, Brandon said, he figured he should get a college degree in business, so he attended a small university in

Washington State. He quickly concluded, though, that he wasn't learning much that he couldn't learn on his own by just doing the work.

So at age nineteen, he launched Indigenous Adventures, drawing tourists from all over. As he takes his fishing clients out to sea, he also tells them about the history of the land and the Tlingit people.

He built his business through social media and by following up with early customers, asking them to please pass the word to friends.

The fishing tourism season lasts only about five months a year, from May into the beginning of October; during the other seven, Brandon works for his tribe as a cultural specialist, interacting with young Tlingit people to grow their sense of identity, creating community events including a workshop of Tlingit song and dance, and educating the non-Tlingit population about his people.

Now in his early twenties, Brandon is married and earning more than $80,000 a year doing work that he believes in and loves. He even brings the teachings about caring for the planet into his fishing business, refusing to give in to customers' pressure to let them keep "breeder fish" that help repopulate the water.

He's a firm believer that a college degree isn't needed to do a lot of the fun, meaningful, and financially rewarding work in the world.

"A lot of my role models don't have college degrees. I went to them and asked, 'How did you get where you are?' It's work ethic, drive. Do something you enjoy, that you're passionate about, and work hard. You'll do well."

OUTDOOR JOBS

In addition to the usual jobs you associate with working outdoors—farming, ranching, construction, firefighting—here are some you might not have considered or realized were open to people without a bachelor's degree.

- *Boat crew and boatyard work.* In addition to the well-paid tugboats that Sam Stanton has worked on, many commercial boats will take on crew who have little to no experience, as long as they're up for learning and hard work. Consider fishing vessels, tall ships, ferries, and cruise ships. When it comes to working on cruise ships, conditions vary widely from one cruise ship to another, and your pay and quarters will be better if you bring a skill to the cruise, such as musician or chef. Sam also says boatyards are always hungry for maintenance and repair people, even those with no experience.

- *Skilled labor.* Most of the jobs you can think of in the trades—electrician, mechanic, plumber—are also done in outdoor settings. It's similar to the same job anywhere else, just a lot prettier and more outdoorsy. National and wilderness parks need tradespeople along with maintenance crews and hospitality employees. To apply for any federal job, including those in national parks and forests and Bureau of Land Management areas, go to usajobs.gov. The search function is extensive and easy to use.

- *Zookeeper.* Are you an animal lover? Zookeeping jobs are plentiful, and they're not solely the scut work of cleaning enclosures, though that's certainly part of it. Zookeepers feed the animals, file regular reports on their well-being, and help educate the public through talks, special events, and interpretive kids' programs.

- *Arborist.* Tree specialists generally make more than gardening generalists or even landscapers, averaging more than $77,000 a year. You can get an associate's degree or certificate in horticulture, or just learn on the job as an assistant to an experienced arborist.

- *Naturalist.* These lovers of the environment understand wild plants and animals. They often assist scientists or keep track of the environment, or they can "interpret," meaning they educate the public about nature. I do this work as a volunteer, but there are paid jobs as well. You can often take courses at community colleges to bolster your knowledge or work as a volunteer to show you have experience. It's also a good idea to take a course to be a certified interpretive guide recognized by the National Association of Interpretation, usually given at community colleges. This means that you know how to educate the public in engaging ways.

- *Archaeology technician.* These assistants to archaeological digs do field assessments and often oversee or participate in the actual digs. Sometimes called archaeology field technicians or archaeological aides, they generally have at least a certificate in the field or an associate's degree. Many job listings do seek candidates with a bachelor's degree, but not all.

- *Fish hatchery technician.* These workers keep track of the health and populations of fish at hatcheries. They also might keep tanks clean and interact with the public.

- *Tour guide.* Guides are employed in all sorts of settings: historical sites, parks, river rafting, fishing, whale watching, zoos, long-distance biking trips, even amusement parks. Being a tour guide is a great fit for people who connect well with others and, for many of these jobs, have a love of nature and/or certain athletic skills. Though no degree is required, you will in many cases need a few certifications. For example, to be a volunteer hiking guide, I needed to be certified in CPR, wilderness first aid, and as a naturalist. Though it wasn't required, I became a certified interpretive guide as well. Some kinds of tour guide jobs require less training, while others, in physically demanding locations, require more. But it's not nearly as time-consuming, expensive, or difficult as getting a bachelor's degree. Salaries for tour guides can run up to $60,000.

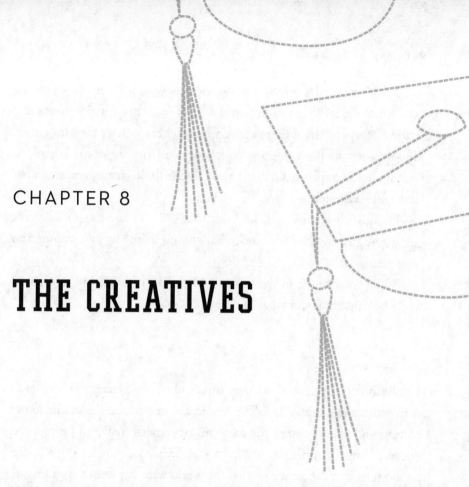

CHAPTER 8

THE CREATIVES

Noah Elbers isn't one of those bread bakers who was kneading dough in his parents' kitchen at the age of twelve. But Noah brings an essential curiosity and big-picture thinking to everything he does, and he had spent many hours during his early years cooking in the farmhouse kitchen of his parents' apple farm. So maybe it's not a big surprise that after building a wood-fired clay oven himself, more as a creative lark than anything, he didn't just learn to make bread—he now owns a bakery that was recently ranked among the top in the nation.

Noah credits the rural New Hampshire community where he spent his formative years, home to many artisans, craftspeople, and entrepreneurs.

"I grew up around makers," Noah said. "The thing I knew and observed growing up was: approach life with the attitude that if you want to have agency and autonomy, you can view the world that way and make things happen."

Noah attended a private high school known for its emphasis on the arts, which he loved but didn't excel at. But reading for assignments and writing essays in the way prescribed by teachers weren't for him either. He said that the push to go to college was a firm one at his school, so he attended Hampshire College, also famous for its arts education. That lasted one semester.

He quickly discovered, he said, that "this is not the thing that's going to light my fire." It wasn't challenging in the ways he wanted to be challenged.

So he went home to the farm and helped his father in the orchard while he thought about what to do next.

•

You'll find creative people all over this book: Tony Santos, the Colorado video editor in chapter 1; Wylie Stateman, one of the leaders in sound editing and sound design for more major movies than can be counted on your fingers and toes, in chapter 2; Erin Carey in chapter 5, the public-relations expert who sailed the world with her family on a private yacht—while making a living doing so; Nina Robins in chapter 6, who found a way to make a living she enjoys while writing slam poetry on the side.

In truth, whether they're entrepreneurs or high school students who work at professional apprenticeships while still attending schools, these are all people who carved out a life without a bachelor's degree, and that's a creative process all by itself. They are, in fact, creating their lives through a wide range of unconventional moves rather than following the usual four-year college path.

So it should be no surprise that creative people are found in just about every field on these pages—and also that many who design their own lives often turn to inherently creative fields such as design, art, entertainment, and cooking.

For the most part, the creative world is kind to people without a four-year college degree. Creative people are generally less tied to old tropes and open to doing things in new ways. Without those attributes, they couldn't create.

But that doesn't mean that working as a creative is something you can just fall into. Most of the people I talked to in the creative fields worked hard at developing their craft and went to great lengths to develop connections and find mentors. So while there is no one way to join these fields—unlike with apprenticeships, I can't give you a list of employers who offer particular jobs—the stories of the creators show you how others have done it and how you can apply many of their strategies to your future.

•

Cooking and baking are essentially creative pursuits. They involve bringing forth a beautiful, delicious product, often in novel or unusual ways that take skill and a never-ending commitment to improvement. For Noah Elbers, his creative pursuit turned out to be making bread in a wood-fired clay oven using natural fermentation.

But in his early days, a lot of Noah's thoughts revolved around how to make a home for himself in ways that would make him feel that he belonged and mattered.

"I was a pretty weird kid," he said. "I loved growing food and planting gardens. I would get so excited about the kinds of tomatoes I was going to grow next season, and canning tomatoes, making tomato sauce.

"I felt like, 'What's wrong with me? Why is this the stuff that really interests me?'"

A creative, break-the-mold neighbor whom Noah admired built a wood-fired clay oven for baking bread. He encouraged Noah to do the same. So he did, just outside the barn on the farm property, and set up two sawhorses with a board across them to use as a table.

At first he baked bread as a hobby, inviting friends over to share. Then he started asking for money. Though the oven remained outside, he began renovating the barn, bit by bit. Wood-fired bread became one of his trademarks; so was his insistence on using only naturally occurring rising agents, such as sourdough starter. He was just twenty years old.

Noah was no natural at bread baking. In fact, his early efforts weren't very good, he said. He needed to learn from the bigger baking community—and he needed a new oven, one fit for professional use. He got that going by sponsoring a workshop by a master maker of clay ovens, teaching others how to do it. He offered rooms to let, camping spots, and food. He charged for the workshop but made no profit. What he gained instead was a place in the baking community, filled with people willing to show him the ropes.

It's not as though Noah has reinvented the art of baking. Bread has been baked for thousands of years, and at heart, Noah said, it's just water, grain, and salt. But turning those simple ingredients into great bread is infinitely complex. The fermenting agent is a living organism that must be managed carefully.

"Bread baking is the pursuit of discovery," he said. "It's not about making it perfect because that never happens. Instead, you're growing this encyclopedia of knowledge that's within you, and it's going to tell you things that you need for the future."

Today Orchard Hill Bakery employs ten people in the bakery and eight part-time staff to package and drive the bread to its destinations. Noah owns nearly five acres of the original fifty-acre farm, where the barn and his baking operation are, and he lives in the farmhouse. He's also come a long way from his early, not-very-good bread; in March 2020, Orchard Hill was named one of the best bread bakeries in the nation by the Food Network. Noah scoffs at that, as good as it is for business. You can't rank bread, he said, and great bread makers can be found all around the country.

Orchard Hill does nearly a million dollars in business each year; Noah pays himself $70,000 of that.

If artisanal bread making is something you might like, it's worth looking up the bakery. Since 2018, Noah has run an apprentice program, providing room and board and $12,000 for the thirteen-month apprenticeship, along with a lot of instruction in baking as part of the team. There are three apprentices each year. Five former apprentices now work as part of the full-time baking staff; others have gone on to bake in other places or have become baking entrepreneurs. Some found that bread wasn't really their thing. From Noah's perspective, that has value too. And at least they didn't spend tens of thousands of dollars in tuition to find out what they don't like.

But mainly, he feels a huge sense of fulfillment by carrying out his original goal of becoming knit into his corner of the world, contributing to it, and in turn being supported by it. Above all, he's proud of creating what sociologist Ray Oldenberg called a "third place." Work is one place, home another. The third place is where people gather between work and home and connect with others. Where they find true community.

●

While it's become common for many people in the arts to pursue a bachelor's degree, it's simply not necessary in almost any of the creative fields.

"People come to our field from wide and varied backgrounds and experiences," Terry Ann Gordon, the president of the Costume Designers Guild Local 892 in Los Angeles, told me. "Love of costume design, the business, and a high level of energy and enthusiasm are crucial. Solid understanding of costuming, production, and design are paramount. But any industrious, hardworking individual can rise quickly through the ranks as a self-starting, self-educated crew member."

This is true not just for creative people but in many of the fields where people without a bachelor's degree make a living. As Gordon pointed out, one of the chief values of a degree program is to create a network of connections and future colleagues. But if that involves four years of college education, you're spending four years and a lot of money to gain a network that you can create on your own. Admittedly, doing it without a ready-made network—which you might or might not get from college—takes some effort. Being a people person helps.

There's also a certain flexibility and fluidity in creative careers, which allows you to use the same abilities in any number of different environments. For example, later in this chapter you'll meet an entertainment-industry makeup designer who does wedding makeup to keep the financial flow steady. Your skills as a set designer can easily translate to interior design with a little extra course study at community colleges or university extensions. The creative field is also where beginners very commonly apprentice to experienced designers—where the pay may be minimal but the experience invaluable in drilling down into your craft and also learning the practicalities and requirements of a business on the spot.

You can be a chef or (as a woman I know did after leaving journalism) create your own gourmet line of jams with unusual flavors. You can design clothing for stage or the fashion trade, or be a custom designer and clothier for rich people. You might be a book author, a content creator for a website, or run your own blog.

•

Franey Miller was a professional fashion photographer by the age of nineteen, with no college or even formal training.

Her parents couldn't afford college, and she was concerned that the courses might constrain her style and creativity.

Franey spent most of her childhood and teen years in Kentucky, where her mother was executive director of the Kentucky Museum of Art and Craft. She first developed an all-consuming passion for photography while she was on a family vacation at the age of eight. Her father gave her a camera, and she hasn't stopped snapping photos since.

She started making money at it while still in school, taking family portraits and photos of the high school seniors.

But it's a long way from local portraits to breaking into the fashion scene. Franey came up with a great way to do it, with or without a college career.

During senior year, while other teenagers were spending their weekends partying or relaxing, Franey was writing emails. Lots and lots of emails.

"Any spare time during the school day, too, I was writing more emails." Messages went out to magazines, agencies, and fashion brands. She had zero connections, and unlike bread baking, fashion photography tends to be a competitive field where networking with other photographers is unlikely to yield much. So instead, hundreds of blind emails went out.

It worked. Some of those people responded, which led to other gigs. She snagged assignments with *New York*, *Bullett*, *Nylon*, and *Oyster* magazines, with Refinery 29 and Anthropologie and designer Mara Hoffman, by being bold enough to break the rules. At the age of seventeen, she walked into the offices of *Bullett* magazine and was able to engage the founder, who happened to be available, in a forty-five-minute conversation. *Oyster* had a no-submissions policy on its website—but Franey submitted anyway and got an assignment. She moved to New York City in 2018 because that's where the jobs were.

It's a constant search for new jobs, but when they come, a single day of work can be a big payout: $2,000, enough for a share in a New York apartment. At this point, she's starting to contact the Los Angeles fashion scene, where she feels there's a growing industry doing fresh things, and more growth. She continues making contacts anywhere she goes.

"I just talk to people when I leave the house," she said. "Talking to them about what I do. And they say, 'I need a photographer' or they know someone who needs photographers."

There are times, though, when Franey feels the need to do something more creative and artistic. Then she'll usually head out into nature, often with friends. Taking photos of people in nature is her favorite pastime. She wants to find a gallery to show her more independent work, and even has plans to produce a book of photographs of plants with medicinal properties. She's applying for grants with the help of her mother, who has written grant proposals as part of her profession.

"Photography saved my life and I'm so happy to be able to do it," Franey said.

•

If music is what calls to you, you probably already know that the path to becoming a performing musician in front of an audience is a dicey one. Some make it; many more don't.

Back when I was a kid living in Yonkers, New York, my brother was in a couple of garage bands. One of those bands included a classmate named Steve Tallarico, a nice guy who would later be known as Steven Tyler of Aerosmith fame. When Steve came over to our house for practice, our mother would always ask, "Steve, *when* are you going to cut that hair of yours?" And Steve would politely reply, "Soon, Mrs. Klein, soon."

Steve became a superstar. My late brother, Marc, became a nurseryman; he'd always loved flowers and plants. I'm sure he would have loved touring the world with his guitar, but he didn't have a natural voice or real flair for music. Perhaps equally important: though he played frequently, he wasn't willing to put in the kind of dedication and determination that Steve brought to it.

As with any other creative pursuit, though, being a literal rock star isn't all there is to joining the music industry. In fact, the actual star performers aren't in the list of the top ten most common jobs in music compiled by the respected Berklee College of Music. Instead, most careers are behind the scenes but offer plenty of creative opportunity: music producer, recording engineer, session musician, artist manager, tour manager, music teacher, booking agent, publicist, composer, and arranger. The only one that requires a degree is teaching music in a public school.

That doesn't mean being uneducated. Composers, for example, need to understand music theory and arrangement. But there are all kinds of private and online lessons and courses for this, and composition software can take you a long way.

How do you get started in any or all of these fields? You may already be a musician—taking lessons, practicing. And you may already be immersed in the music world, listening to music and making decisions from that about your tastes. If you already have these skills, you can start looking for chances to build them and use them professionally.

It helps that networking is natural among musicians; even in high school, you should be meeting other musicians, practicing with them, and working with them. Networking is how you find out about gigs. Put yourself out there; a teen band touting itself on my local Nextdoor drew a lot of interest. Cultivate relationships at local restaurants and cafés, even ones that don't offer live music right now (maybe especially if they don't offer live music). Offer to play once a week for the donations you'll get and the exposure. Bring contact cards and make them easily available to your listeners. If you're good, chances are that people will ask if you're available. That's how I found the guitarist to perform at a big party I gave.

Then you might build out from that exposure into related fields that give you more variety of experience or fill your schedule to give you full-time paying work.

Ben Perlstein's résumé includes most of the jobs in the Berklee top ten, but he also has been a performing musician. He'll tell you that all of this is absolutely possible without a college degree and that no two paths are quite the same.

•

Ben had been accepted to a college in St. Paul, Minnesota. Money wasn't a problem; his parents were ready to pay, and they certainly wanted him to go.

But once he graduated from the private Wisconsin boarding school he'd attended—a school where, he says, if it didn't look like students were going to college, they would be expelled—he decided college wasn't for him.

Ben had a leg up in one industry: music. He played guitar, bass, and keyboard as a kid and very young man. In his high school days, friends from his hometown introduced him to a group of kids his age who had a punk band and were already performing in a few local places. Ben joined the band and, out of necessity, started booking them into the veterans' hall and other venues so they'd get to play before an audience and be noticed. As a result, he already had experience booking acts. It was the perfect way for him to maintain his involvement in music and promote musicians whose work he especially appreciated.

"There was a band from Florida I thought was really cool, and I wanted to book them. I reached out to someone I knew in the music business," he said. "He ended up connecting me with the owner of the Globe East Nightclub in Milwaukee, and the owner ended up hiring me."

People at the Globe showed him how the system worked, what the venue scene looked like, and how to put on shows. With the help of musician friends, he quickly developed a feel for "which bands were cool.

"All that was kind of my college, learning on the fly."

Ben did try college during those years but lasted only a semester. He says he later was diagnosed with ADHD, and an earlier diagnosis might have helped him stick with school. But he had other interests than what he was learning in classes. He then tried college again and left after a semester and a half, this time because his band, The Benjamins, got a record deal in the year 2000. That gave them the money to go on tour.

The Benjamins lasted only a year and a half on the road. Some members found the touring more than they could take. Ben joined another band in Minneapolis, where the band's manager recruited him into the talent management agency where he worked. Ben was put in charge of the band Soul Asylum, which found big-time fame with its Grammy award–winning hit "Runaway Train." Ben was tasked with their day-to-day management as well as managing their tours and working with very large venues.

"I hadn't had that experience," he said. "I learned everything there."

His work included managing tours for the reggae musician Matisyahu, a Hasidic Jew at the time. Ben toured with Matisyahu for two years, handling all the usual aspects of running a tour but with the added complications of Matisyahu's religious requirements: he and his family ate only kosher food; he could not touch women other than his wife; and he could not perform during the Sabbath, from Friday evening to Saturday evening.

Ben went on to manage other musicians, including Tommy Stinson, and he comanaged Stinson's reunited Replacements, a celebrated punk band that had been banned for life from *Saturday Night Live* after its members got drunk while performing on the show and engaged in some unacceptable antics (like one member dropping an F-bomb). More than twenty years later, the band reunited for a two-year sellout tour. But this time, Ben wasn't traveling with a group; he was hiring the tour managers to do that.

"We headlined shows like Coachella and made a lot of people happy," he said. "More people started returning my phone calls after that."

Ben was hired by a management company in New York but quit two years later, wanting to do something more creative.

"I reached out to the owner of a music festival in Chicago. He said he had a need for a creative director. And he wanted me to help him build it," Ben said. "I got a budget to hire writers and content creators. I helped oversee creative marketing. We opened a pop-up restaurant for three months, and I did the décor to make it look like a circus freak show." (There's that set design for you, without any education in the field.)

Ben said that his annual earnings varied during all these activities, from about $50,000 to a high of $150,000 for the Replacements reunion tour.

His life was exciting and varied. But not everything about it was positive. Drugs and alcohol are "so much a part of the scene," he said, and he got caught up in it at one point, as did a longtime musician friend from high school. "We overcame it together," Ben said. "I got him into treatment about ten years ago."

Ben isn't just a manager. He still has the music in him and sings and plays guitar and drums.

"I'm in a band inasmuch as I make songs and I make recordings and I have a couple of collaborators," he said. "It's more of a hobby."

Now in his forties, Ben recently took a full-time job as manager of productions at a historic, seven-thousand-square-foot venue in

Milwaukee. But he's also been working on making the switch to music production and engineering.

He has zero regrets about not getting a bachelor's degree. "There's no traditional path for where I went," he said. "If you know in your gut you should do something, then do it."

•

I can't tell you how to be a famous actor with a mansion, a spot on the Academy Awards red carpet, and an entourage. If I knew the answer to that, I'd probably be doing it, as long as they let me write too.

But even more than with music, the vast majority of jobs in the film and television industry are what's known as "below the line," which for the most part means anyone who's not the producer, director, screenwriter, casting director, or principal cast. These people edit the movies or do costumes or makeup. They make up the lighting crew, production crews, and work as film editors, makeup artists, costume designers, cinematographers, and so forth. Many of the positions are filled by college graduates, but a degree is not really required for any of them. The main thing people want to know is if you have the skills for the job.

You can gain many of those skills in private courses, community colleges, online tutorials, and by just plain working at it. But getting picked up for jobs can be a challenge, and that's true for college grads as well. So I've created a separate list in this chapter, culled from people in the industry, of ways to break in.

What I hope to see in the future are more high school and adult-education classes to prepare people for these careers. You can find them at some of the performing-arts high schools, but usually more as an afterthought.

One exception: In 2022, with the urging and assistance of actor George Clooney, the Los Angeles Unified School District opened the Roybal School of Film and Television Production, which specifically designs its training around below-the-line careers. The founding partners include a lineup of major producers of film and television, including Sony Pictures, Walt Disney Studios, Paramount, and Netflix. The studios provide internships and apprenticeships, not to mention immediate contacts in the industry, so that students can go straight from high school to well-paid union jobs.

It's not just happening in the Hollywood area, though it's helpful to attend school in an area that has an entertainment industry to provide jobs, guidance, and support. In Nashville, the heartland of country music, Pearl-Cohn Entertainment Magnet High School offers an academy in audio and audiovisual production and has its own record label, with connections to a major record company. Students already are landing internships at recording companies and getting paid through part-time jobs doing video for local organizations.

It bears repeating: join Facebook groups in your area of interest, where you can meet people, make friends, learn about the careers, and perhaps find some connections for jobs. There are groups for just about every field. Search also for chat rooms and in-person groups in your area. There's no such thing as having a positive relationship with too many people.

•

Facebook groups are, in fact, what Krystle Feher has found most useful in becoming a makeup artist in the entertainment field.

Krystle, who grew up in a suburb of Cleveland, says she never had the desire to go to college.

"I knew from an early age that wasn't the path I wanted to go on," she said. "It would be not only a waste of my time but a massive waste of money."

She was drawn to movies, especially horror films, and that's what attracted her to the world of cosmetics.

"*The Wizard of Oz* just floored my brain," she said. "How do you use makeup to make a person look like a monkey who's still human?

"I'd always been artistic. When I realized you could turn people into monsters, that was it."

Krystle knew she needed training, however. There are numerous schools that focus solely on cinematic makeup design. Krystle found one in Los Angeles and moved there in 2008.

Krystle opted for the full twelve-month program, which cost about $14,000—a good chunk of money but a lot less expensive than a college education. Tuition included the makeup kit, which at the professional level is a hefty investment, providing everything a makeup artist needs for about 85 percent of the jobs they might ever undertake. Krystle attended classes for two or three days a week, eight hours each day, learning everything from makeup for the fashion world to creating prosthetics. The teachers were terrific, she said—one so accomplished he left midsession to do the elaborate makeup for *The Lion King* on Broadway.

But it wasn't through school connections that Krystle got her first jobs—it was through Craigslist. Now, she says, chat rooms, online groups, and local in-person interest groups are a more popular way to find openings.

"It's not *what* you know," she said. "It's *who* you know. Every job is about networking and connecting."

Her first job was doing makeup for the album cover for a metal band. "I did a photo shoot in an old church and put eyeliner on these guys. It was really fun, and I made maybe fifty dollars."

As she built her résumé, she found work in television, film, and commercials.

She returned to Ohio for a while to learn skincare at another esthetician school. From there, she went to Boston, where, she says, her film career took off.

"Boston has exploded in the film world," she said. "I left in 2016, and it's grown exponentially since then."

She got her first film there when a friend of her sister's brought her on for a very short movie. She did natural-looking makeup and sometimes some "eye bruising." But she learned some essential skills on the job about movie makeup—such as how to break down a script and find a look for each character.

"What I like to do is read the entire script through once, and then I go back and I tab each character and which scenes they're in, and then from there you're designing a look," she said. "I will digitally draw what I visualize and then work with the director."

Over time, Krystle built a résumé that allowed her to join the entertainment industry union for makeup artists and hair stylists, which gave her access to even more jobs. Not that the union was the source of those jobs. "You still have to find your own work," she said. "But it allows you to work on a much bigger range of projects and a higher tier of work. You can't get a job on a Marvel movie if you're not a member of the union. And you're guaranteed a certain minimum pay, depending on what the tier is."

Krystle landed a good job in New York City for FX studios, helping to build the prosthetics for a TV show. It was right up her alley—coming full circle to what first drew her to the field.

Eventually, her big break came: working on the twenty-episode return of the reality show *Supernanny*, in which a professional nanny helps parents with their child-rearing problems. She traveled all over the nation with the show, until the COVID-19 pandemic shut down production.

At her height, her earnings reached $1,200 a day, though Krystle says $600 a day is more common.

During the pandemic shutdown, Krystle moved to Florida and was able to support herself, but not at the level as before the virus. She hustled to fill her hours in by doing wedding makeup and designing greeting cards.

Then in 2023, she moved to Nashville, Tennessee, where she has found her happy place doing makeup for musicians in that active performance and recording scene.

"Build your community and use your community," she said. And don't forget: "If you are interacting with and helping others, they are more apt to help you."

If there's one great piece of advice that should work for finding your way in the creative world, it's this from Amy B. Scher's father: "Just *try* to get in the door."

And that's what she did. In fact, she opened a few different doors until life—and health problems—showed her where she belonged. Now in her early forties, she is a successful author, writer, and teacher who makes six figures a year.

One door Amy never seriously considered was college.

"I had a very hard time in high school," she said. "I felt so much pressure. I'm more of a creative."

Amy grew up in Ojai, a Southern California town known for its emphasis on the arts and for its easygoing ways. She describes her parents as "kind of hippies."

After high school, she worked as a nanny for a while. Even then, she said, she was making $20 an hour, more than any of her friends, including college grads. Her employers were wealthy and would even pay for Amy to travel with them.

She followed that up by training to get a license to sell insurance. "I hated the sales part but loved the social part," she said.

She then was hired as a newsroom assistant at the local newspaper. A lot of it was scut work, getting the information for listings on new births and activities in the area. But soon they let Amy write a couple of real stories, which kicked off her writing career. She used those skills to get a job in marketing for Harley-Davidson, a position that on paper required a college degree. But Amy's outgoing personality sold the company on hiring her.

Amy's forward momentum came to a halt when at age twenty-seven, she said, she got very sick with chronic Lyme disease. The illness was debilitating; she had trouble walking without falling down, and doctors seemed unable to counter the disease successfully. After a year of failed medical treatments, Amy found herself out of options in the United States. Desperate, she traveled to India for an experimental stem-cell treatment that she says cured her—for a little while.

"While I was in India, I had a contact who had a website with a blog, and I asked if I could use their platform to tell my story," she said. "I started blogging and was able to use that experience to pitch a couple of articles for online publications."

When some of her symptoms started showing up again a year after treatment, Amy turned inward to discover a route to full healing that involved examining how the mind affected health. "I was such a people pleaser and a perfectionist," she said. She found her own way back to full health in 2010, when she turned thirty.

She guest-blogged about her healing journey, then wrote a couple of online articles and a self-published memoir that consisted mostly of her previous blog posts. Through that, she was able to find a literary agent. Amy believes that her marketing experience was one of the things the agent found attractive; a book's sales depend heavily on the author's ability to promote it. The agent was then able to get her a contract with a small publisher to write about how to heal when nothing else works. That became the first of a three-part series of books on healing—which led to a contract with a major publisher to write a memoir about her struggles with and eventual victory over illness.

Along the way, Amy worked hard on marketing her books, sending out videos to promote them. "I think because I didn't have a college degree, I was more inventive," she said.

She also wrote travel articles, which naturally led to assignments for *more* travel articles. When I spoke to her, Amy was at work on a fifth book—a travel guide.

Another great thing happened to Amy while in India: she met the woman who would become her wife. They now live in New York.

Amy's creative life has expanded as well. Her memoir, *This Is How I Save My Life*, was published by Simon & Schuster in 2018 and became a bestseller, featuring glowing blurbs from *Eat, Pray, Love* author Elizabeth Gilbert and Harvard Medical School's Sanjiv Chopra. She's written for the *Washington Post*, CNN, and the *Los Angeles Review of Books*. Freelancing for Thrillist led to a nine-month travel project on queer-friendly destinations in the United States. She teaches writing classes as well as health-related classes based on her method of healing.

It all started with the people who were willing to give her a shot at writing even though she lacked a college degree. Her people skills, writing talent, and marketing knowledge did the rest.

She explored her options, took advantage of what was presented to her by life, and learned about her natural skills and what she likes doing.

"Once somebody validates you, it means so much," she said. "But first you really to have to believe in yourself."

MAKING IT IN FILM AND TELEVISION

Don't run out of the movie theater or switch to another streaming show right after the final scene. Take a few minutes to look at the full list of credits at the end of a production. You'll see that the director and cast are just the tip of the iceberg in filmmaking. Remember, there are a lot more jobs, and a lot more ways to gain entry, in the film business than the handful of glamourous careers people know from the awards ceremonies.

Here are just a few of those roles and details on how you might be able to break into the film and television entertainment industry:

- *Check out the Assistant Directors Training Program*, with programs in Los Angeles and New York City, run by the Directors Guild of America. It's competitive to get into, and not as glamorous as it sounds, but it is paid. Days are long, and there's a lot of gofer (go for this, go for that) duty and delivering actors to the set. In addition to the on-the-job training, courses are available that help you build knowledge and skills, and you get guaranteed admission to the Guild, which can grow your network of potential mentors tremendously. Applicants must have at least two years of college and/or work and should have a demonstrated interest in filmmaking.
- *Contact the unions, studios, production companies, and academies* of

the kinds of work that interest you—film editing, makeup, hair styling, and so on—and see if you can get a job there. *Any* job, including taking orders for coffee. Being in their offices and interacting exposes you to the professionals in the field who might be willing to look at what you've done and hire you or refer you to someone else. Susanna A. Song (you'll learn more about her in the chapter on community colleges, chapter 12) got her start as a costume designer by working just two days at the Costume Designers Guild. That was enough to earn her a boatload of connections and led to her first job in a production, which then led to referrals for other jobs. The International Academy of Television Arts and Sciences recently listed an opening for an Emmy Awards assistant and did not list college education as a requirement.

- *Sign up for a temp agency that serves the film and television industry.* You might just be typing letters, but if you do solid work and impress someone with your personality and competence, you might be offered a permanent job that leads to greater things.

- *Consider film editing*, which requires some level of training even for the lowliest of assistants. Possible employers will want to see that you're familiar with AVID, one of the main digital editing platforms. You can get started on YouTube, but eventually you'll want a certificate; search online for schools near you. UCLA Extension gives a series of three classes leading to certification; it's not cheap, at about $2,500, but that's a lot less money than a year at just about any college you can name. You can also look into remote courses. But here's another promising route: in the past couple of years, the Motion Picture Editors Guild brought back its apprenticeship program, which does not require college.

- *Ask around on social media if anyone knows someone looking for a production assistant (PA).* Many a Hollywood veteran has begun her career as a PA. It's a low-level job basically doing anything that's needed, but it gains you exposure. Once you land the first gig and do a good job, more opportunities generally follow.

- *Join Facebook groups connected to your interest in film.* Learn from those who already are making it, and ask questions, show your stuff, and impress people who might lead you to jobs.
- *Regularly comb job websites specifically tailored to the entertainment industry*, including Backstage Crew, Creative Pool, EntertainmentCareers.Net, and UTA Jobs List, and look under "Assistant Level Positions."
- *Search for internships on Showbiz*: showbizjobs.com/internships. This website posts short-term gigs in just about every aspect of filmmaking and has listings for regular jobs as well.
- *Contact people in the film industry* whose work you especially admire. Be prepared to talk about their work in a way that shows you've paid attention and drawn something from it. Offer to work for them as an assistant doing anything they need at very low pay. You'll build tremendous new insight and skills, meet people in the business, and quite possibly end up with a mentor.
- *Build a network of friends in a similar position.* When one succeeds, they'll often bring you along or let you know about openings they're too busy to take. Be prepared to do the same for your friends.

HOW TO BECOME A WRITER

You're probably already a writer if you're reading this section. Maybe you write poetry or do journalism for the campus newspaper or journal a lot and have ideas for a novel. Whatever it is, what readers care about—as well as publishers and agents—is whether you have something worthwhile to say and you say it well, not whether you've attended a four-year college.

Employers, literary agents, and publishing houses pretty much care about the same thing, but it can be a little more complicated when you don't have a degree and you're just starting out. How do they know you can write? That you're accurate with facts? That you meet deadlines?

I doubt the contract for me to write this book had anything to do with my degree. What mattered was that I was a veteran journalist for a major publication, that I had covered education for most of my career, and that I already had written about life without a college degree. The editors at the publishing house knew they could trust my reporting and writing abilities and that my English usage was pretty good. I'd already written a book, though a very different one, so they knew that long-form writing was within my skill set.

The pathways to fiction and poetry writing are different from those in journalism, essays, and the like. If you set out to write the next Harry Potter or Hunger Games series, your chances are as good as those of anyone who has a degree. Likewise, literary journals are going to judge what's on the page. They're not interested in judging you or your education level.

It's not a bad idea to be able to handle multiple kinds of writing. Few writers do just one. Horror novelist Stephen King has written many essays, as well as an excellent book about writing.

The first and most important thing? Write and get published, which usually means doing it for little or even no pay in the beginning. Look at Amy B. Scher, whose story is highlighted in this chapter. I'm awed by the number of books she's traditionally published in a short time. But she didn't just start out writing books. She used many experiences to build skills and clips and develop a body of work.

As a rapacious content-generating machine, the internet also has made it much easier to get your words to the public. It has increased the number of publications of all types and allows you to start your own publication as well as to self-publish e-books at minimal cost. The same is true of film and music.

Here are some ideas for getting started as a writer:

- Offer to provide pieces free or at minimal cost to platforms that already have blogs. Or start your own blog and send out word via social media.

- Join writing groups on Facebook and LinkedIn—there are many. You can look specifically for groups that offer writing jobs, but you also should be part of a bigger community to learn about the craft and the business. When I spent a few years as a freelancer rather than as a staff writer, it was a Facebook group (that no longer exists) that made all the difference in showing me how to transition my existing skills to a new world.

- Look for an in-person writing group in which people critique each other's work. What you'll need is a group in which people are not afraid to criticize. If it's a polite, no-hurt-feelings group, you're not going to learn much. You might have better luck with some online writing groups that offer community, resources, and, in some cases, valuable critique: Scribophile and Critique Circle, which provide active critique from other writers; Reddit's writing thread; and Writing.com.

- Take community college classes in journalism or expository writing. They'll teach you skills and you'll have something to put on your résumé. You might be able to publish in the school's literary magazine. I'll risk irritating some people and say that community colleges are often not as useful for creative writing classes because your classmates generally don't know more than you do, aren't trained in doing the kind of specific critiquing that will help improve your writing, and are naturally leery about saying anything negative. Also, the classes are often too large.

- Ask your local newspaper or other publication if you can work for them as a student (or beginning) journalist for minimum pay. As Amy did, you might start out doing little more than gathering lists—activities in town on the weekend or police reports for the crime blotter. But opportunities invariably arise to do some actual writing—especially if you ask. Don't let the editing process discourage you; know that the edits you'll receive will be invaluable in helping you improve.

- Offer to work as a researcher/apprentice in author groups or with an author you particularly admire. If you're highly organized and good at research, there's nothing like working with a pro and seeing the process up close.

- Join an online writing association. I particularly like Paragraph, at paragraphny.com, which for a $25-a-month virtual membership offers craft talks and occasional access to editor critique or to pitching literary agents. There also are seminars on how to pitch your writing to editors, writing groups for connecting with other writers who share your specific interests, and discounts on low-cost writing workshops.

- Read. Maybe there's the rare writer who can just churn out informed, beautifully written material without being a big reader, but almost all writers are committed readers at heart. Good writing enters our minds and influences our writing even if we don't realize it's happening. If you're writing about nonfiction topics, inform yourself by reading from a variety of sources and keeping up on current events. If you're applying for a job, employers want to know that you are a knowledgeable, thinking person, whether the topic is politics or rap. Be prepared to talk about your favorite books; if you don't read any, you won't have any.

- Please use spellcheck and other programs to check your spelling and English usage. Sloppy writing and poor grammar send an immediate bad impression.

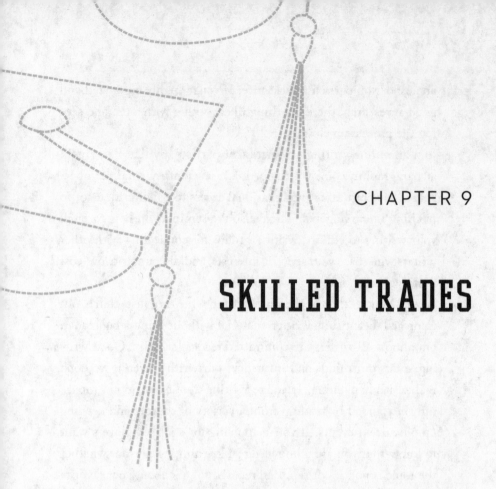

CHAPTER 9

SKILLED TRADES

Probably no other high school does education in the skilled trades—plumber, builder, electrician, mechanic, and so forth—the way Sheboygan South High does. But I wish more did.

You met Sheboygan South counselor Stephen Schneider in chapter 1. His high school tried to persuade all of its students to go to college until it found out that no matter how hard it pushed, half of its seniors weren't moving on to higher education. In other words, the counseling program was ignoring half its students.

So the counselors decided to do something unusual: change the message. Instead of "College, college, college," they told students, "We exist to give you as much advantage as we can in whatever future you plan." Skilled trades would no longer be the second-rate, also-ran future for students; it would be one of two major prongs.

It's more than a motto. Each year of high school at Sheboygan South has a theme. For freshmen, it's about transitioning into high school and understanding that these are the years that set them up for success. In sophomore year, the theme is exploring, discovering, and being exposed to the different possibilities beyond high school and having students think about what they're good at and like doing. Juniors start working on a plan. They can always change it, but the idea is to start moving in some kind of direction. The juniors then run a meeting about their plans that parents attend and counselors moderate.

Senior year is when students start putting their plans into action. Those who've chosen the trades go on a bus tour to look at various employers in their area who need skilled workers. Even better, the school has set up ninety-hour apprenticeships, called co-ops, that allow students to experience the different kinds of work and workplaces and see what interests them the most. These co-ops are guaranteed educational experiences, not low-paid scut work, and students are paid. There's also a more intensive two-year apprenticeship program for junior and senior year, for students who want to build skills in a particular field. On senior signing day, seniors gather to talk about their plans for the first years after high school, and the counseling office verifies these plans. Those planning to take jobs immediately sign a commitment with their future employers there as witnesses.

Schneider talked about how the co-op program kept one student from being a dropout. Remote learning during the pandemic had been especially tough for this student, and when school opened in person again, he wasn't showing up.

"I was calling him and saying, 'Colin, you have to come in.'" Academics simply weren't Colin's strong point, so Schneider tempted him back to school with a co-op. Colin liked his first one so much that he did several—Schneider calls him the "king of the co-ops." Colin then went on to an apprenticeship and had a job straight out of college at a local company making $22 an hour to start, fixing machinery. He rented his own place and bought a car. His company then paid for him to attend community college for certification in electromechanics, making better money.

Cody Burrows, another student in the Sheboygan trades program, says college never felt like the right thing for him. "I'm more of a hands-on kind of guy," he said. Doing co-ops, which took a quarter of his school year, brought him into the manufacturing, orthodontics, and auto mechanic worlds.

When we talked in 2022, Cody was a senior at Sheboygan South and was doing his fourth co-op in the service department of an auto dealership.

"The other thing I like about co-ops, you can try it, and if you don't like it, you don't have to stick with it," he said. "You learn early on what you don't like." He'd already discovered that he didn't like orthodontics work—too much sitting in a chair working with tiny pieces of equipment waiting for robots to do their part.

Fixing cars was something else, though. He could keep moving, and the work wasn't rote. "There's never a right or wrong answer because cars are full of mysteries," he said.

His stint at the dealership went so well that his boss asked if he'd like to continue. Cody was about to move up into a yearlong apprenticeship. His goal was to move into a higher-level apprenticeship that would give him a $5,000 set of tools, and then get a full-time job at that dealership.

"I love the people there, my boss, everyone there is amazing."

He liked his high school courses, too, the ones in career tech, especially metallurgy—"metals fabrication at the highest level," Cody explained. One of the things he loves most about his field is constantly learning new things—a view that runs counter to many people's idea of skilled trades as work set in place without growth.

Not for a moment did Cody strike me as complacent or settling for a less-than-great future. He sounded as excited about learning new things as any English major jumping into a Shakespeare seminar course.

"I have a five-year goal," Cody said, an idea he got from his boss: get the certification to become a master technician for Nissan cars so that he's able to do the bigger jobs on any part of a car. He'd recently bought a 1995 Nissan coupe—his first car and his first big project in auto mechanics.

Sheboygan is an extreme example of high schools that are heeding the call to bring back what used to be called "shop classes"—essentially, training for a skilled trade. Many of the people doing these jobs talk about how they're making more money than classmates who graduated college, without the time and cost required for college.

Bringing more hands-on work to high school doesn't just get students ready for paying jobs. For kids who like to work with their hands or solve mechanical problems, career programs often keep them from dropping out.

I'll admit to having concerns, though. Vocational education has a troubled history that a lot of people would like to forget—one in which Black and Latino students were routinely herded into the trades rather than the college track, no matter where their interests and talents lay. It's crucial that safeguards be in place to prevent that.

Sheboygan South counselors believe that long-range planning and bringing parents into the process early on help counter any attempts to herd students against their inclinations. It's certainly a huge improvement, but it still isn't giving students the range of choices or information they need. It doesn't break free from the three options most high school students are introduced to by school counselors: college, military, or the trades.

People will be changing jobs and fields more often in the future than they did in my father's day or in mine. The opportunities for people without a bachelor's degree are expanding every month, it seems, and even those who are college-bound should be getting more exposure to different fields and work experiences before starting college. How about work in marketing or creative fields, the tourism industries, entrepreneurship, or management? We're sending students out into the world with too limited a view of what's available.

Still, skilled trades are hot right now, with more openings than qualified people to take them. The baby boomers have been retiring from those jobs, and their skills were so honed that it takes two and sometimes three beginners to replace them. But be aware that outsourcing and real estate downturns can create a glut of workers in the future, and the effect of robotics is yet unknown. Yes, there's a predicted shortage of welders, but so many schools are churning out new welders, it's unclear how long that superheated demand will last.

Work in skilled trades can make for a satisfying career with a stable future and opportunity for growth. But check to make sure that the field you're interested in is projected to grow over the next decade—and make at least preliminary plans for how to skill up if this one goes flat or if you want to take it to another level.

To check out the full list of occupations, their expected growth rate, and pay ranges (which are based on averages at a point in time, and could be off by a significant amount), go to the Occupational Outlook Handbook at bls.gov/ooh/occupation-finder.htm.

I like programs like Sheboygan's primarily for what Cody mentioned: instead of just randomly picking a trade, students get a chance to explore several of them. The post–high school programs for learning these skills are much less expensive and time-consuming than a four-year college— and plentiful. At community colleges (see chapter 12), there are fast-track certificate programs that take weeks or months as well as associate's degree programs, which are the least expensive route you can take for higher education. Take a look at some of the more unusual programs, such as avionics at Pima Community College in Tucson, Arizona.

Private trade schools are more expensive than community colleges but much less expensive than a four-year degree, and these often have more extensive choices than public colleges. Make sure to check these schools carefully, though: they should be accredited and have job-placement services. Find current students and alumni to ask about their experiences, and talk to employers in the field about whether they would hire people from that school.

•

Underwater welder Errol Gritten is among those warning young people away from private trade schools that might be promising too much. Not the welding schools; those are doing a good job of turning out people who have at least some skills in their field. But diving schools, he said, will promise new high school grads that by spending $40,000 to train as a commercial diver, they'll be making serious bank. All but a few don't, he said, and end up leaving the career disappointed and a lot poorer.

Welding is the field everyone's talking about these days. It's relatively well paid, and a longtime shortage of welders was expected to reach 400,000 in the United States in 2024, according to the American Welding Society.

As a result, community colleges and adult education programs all over the country have been adding welding courses. And now, at least two high schools in Illinois, Elgin and Hampshire, not only teach welding but have programs set up so that students can earn their welding certification while they earn their diplomas.

As an underwater welder, Errol is at the apex of the welding industry. Underwater welding requires high levels of expertise in commercial diving and top-level welding skills using highly specialized equipment. At age thirty-eight, he's earning $150,000 plus stellar benefits. He could make a higher salary, he said, but he likes the freedom he has in his job with Phoenix International; its emphasis on safety, professionalism, and teamwork; and the ability to work from home some of the time, planning welding projects and living with his wife and daughter in a stunningly picturesque area of Montana near one of the entrances to Yellowstone National Park. He also gets to travel the world about half the time, to more countries than he can recall, for projects from repairing ship parts to joining pipelines.

Errol grew up in upstate New York but moved to Montana just as he was reaching adulthood. The son of a carpenter, he became adept at using his hands starting at a young age. "I kind of grew up on a job site," he said.

He went to college to study mechanical engineering, but after three semesters realized it was not for him. "I don't like being behind a desk," he said.

It wasn't an easy decision to make at that time, the early 2000s. "Everyone was pushing us, if you don't go to college, you're nothing," he said.

Errol went back to carpentry work and saved money to go to South Africa to spend time with extended family. He worked at a dive shop that gave him lessons. He liked it so well that he came home to Montana, saving the money he made in carpentry work to attend dive school in Seattle for a commercial diving license. He looked into becoming an instructor, but the pay wasn't great, and neither was the challenge.

Errol then was offered an unusual shot at a great career: he was hired right away by an underwater welding company that was willing to teach him the welding part of the job.

"I got lucky, and I worked hard," he said. "I would say about 95 percent of kids out of dive school don't have the luck."

But there were downsides to that first company. It wasn't as safety oriented as it should have been and hadn't invested in the twelve-dollar clips needed to keep crucial equipment attached properly. The result? The equipment came off, leaving him without air. He was pulled up to the boat, but he had blacked out and developed aspiration pneumonia with a fever of 105 degrees.

That's why he switched to Phoenix International and why he said that, when he's putting together a welding team for a project, "If I have anyone who's unsafe or not a team member who cares about everyone else, they're not allowed on the team."

There's a huge demand for underwater welders, he said. But it's not easy to find divers who have at least a decent amount of welding training; better yet is some work experience welding. Another problem is that too many of the young divers don't have the work ethic needed for the intense hours and weeks of completing a job.

"The first couple of years, that's where you really hone your skills," Errol said. "You need to make the trade your life. My first year I worked nine months straight without a day off. I loved it and wanted to learn as much as I could as quick as I could." His team members pushed each other to improve. "We all cared for each other and wanted to learn more. Now the people we get just want to know how much they'll make."

Errol does incredibly difficult work that requires planning, problem solving, attention to detail, and a tremendous work ethic. It commands huge respect from those in the know. And he feels comfortable with his decision that college wasn't right for him.

Asked what he would like to see his preschool daughter do, he joked, "I would love for her to be a doctor or an astronaut."

He then got more serious: "As long as she's doing something she loves, then I'm happy. As long as she has a drive and a passion in her life."

•

One rap on skilled trades has been that, for too long, the fields have been tougher to crack for women and people of color. Another is that although these workers make more than many college grads from the get-go, over time many people with a bachelor's degree earn substantially more. But that's starting to change.

One union isn't just training new people and diversifying the workforce. It's also starting to redefine college and the career arc for manual work.

The Finishing Trades Institute, the education arm of the International Union of Painters and Allied Trades, has branches all over the country that train and certify apprentices as painters, drywall finishers, and glaziers. But more recently, it's added a new twist: while many academic community colleges are beefing up their skilled trades curricula, the institute has added general education courses and been granted the accreditation to award associate's degrees that can be used to transfer to four-year colleges. It's all at a nominal price that beats just about any public community college—a couple hundred dollars per course, after financial aid that's extended to almost every student.

Not only that, but the next goal is to open a trade high school that then seamlessly moves students into the apprenticeship associate's program and, for those who eventually want one, a bachelor's degree program as well.

That might sound crazy. Isn't the whole point of skilled trades that people *don't* need a four-year degree? But John Burcaw, director of academic education at the Finishing Trades Institute of the Upper Midwest in Minnesota, explained that this would be a specialized college for students who want management jobs in the construction trades. It would transform the skilled trades from being a job to a growth career.

"The whole reason we started the degree program was employers who were saying they need good front-office people," he said. "In my day, it was, you'll be an apprentice, then you'll be a journey worker, you'll work for thirty years, and you'll retire. Now you'll have a lattice of opportunities if you want them: safety director, entrepreneur, project manager, construction manager."

Graduates from the school, who will be skilled workers themselves, will understand the work and the projects much better than someone with only a generic business degree. And, should construction run into sour periods, their management experience will help them land safely in other front-office jobs.

Meanwhile, Burcaw has seen definite upticks in the number of people who want to become apprentices and employers who want to hire them. It's taken awhile to build this kind of appreciation for the work skilled craftspeople do.

"There was that business of looking down their noses by people who make less money and have fewer benefits," he said.

The program starts in high school, with very limited hours. It's not about learning a trade yet. Instead, students get exposure to available careers and learn financial literacy. Instructors prep them for the real world, teaching them how to produce professional-looking résumés and impressive cover letters and conducting mock job interviews with them. I'd argue that these are skills all high school students should be receiving. Far too few understand how to budget, manage their money, or apply for a job, even years into their careers. That includes college grads.

After high school, the trainees start in paid apprenticeships with employers, not only learning their trade from longtime experts but also receiving training at the institute a couple of days a week and receiving college credit for their hours. They're paid about $28 an hour plus medical and retiree benefits. And when they move on to the journeyman level, pay increases to about $44 an hour. Demand is heavy enough that many are earning six figures, Burcaw said, easily outearning their college-graduate peers.

Burcaw is also proud that in highly paid union work long dominated by white males, about half of his trainees are women and/or people of color.

Among them is Kailee Schminkey, who was certain she wanted to be a nurse until she spent a couple of years in nursing school. "Nursing was my passion. I always wanted to help people and be the difference in a lot of people's lives." Kailee was living at home but paying the expenses of school herself, which totaled $3,000 to $5,000 per semester. Her job as a personal care attendant for $12 an hour wasn't quite getting her through, and then the pandemic hit, which required a break from work and school. Besides, nursing school was hard work with tough standards. The stress was making her sick to her stomach.

When she first turned to the Finishing Trades Institute, her plan was to make some decent money, save up, and return to school for her nursing degree. Instead, she found that she loved being a commercial painter—and her stress levels plummeted.

"I never thought I would enjoy and have passion for a construction job as much as I do," Kailee said.

She was apprenticed to a commercial painting company, learning most of her skills on the job and some of them in classes at the institute.

"I thought, *It can't be that hard; it's just painting*," Kailee said. "I didn't know anything. I didn't know that you spray paint on the walls. I didn't know ceilings got painted. When they said do the 'cutting in' in the bathroom, I didn't know what they meant. That's outlining a room and then you roll in between the lines."

There were no other women on the crew. One who joined decided to become an electrician instead. Another wasn't taking it seriously, repeatedly showing up late for work. She didn't last long.

During her three years of apprenticeship, Kailee's pay rose from $20 an hour to $43, always with health and retirement benefits. Now at age twenty-four, she's become a journey worker—after her May 2023 graduation from the institute with an associate's degree—and will stay with the same company.

She likes the people and has been treated well, with her pay rising to journey level before she graduated. And the pace and physical work suit her. "It's go, go, go, get as much work done as you can. It's constant moving, and the day goes by really fast."

But Kailee's educational and career ambitions have grown. She now plans to get her bachelor's degree through the institute and to become a project or contractor manager, jobs for which incomes rise well into the six figures. She's at ease being the only woman on her crew; it's other crews they sometimes work with that have caused occasional trouble. Mostly it's men staring at her to the point where she feels uncomfortable. One time it was a man saying something inappropriate, so she complained to a supervisor, and it was handled.

"I personally feel almost empowered because I'm the only female at my company and am a lot of the time one of the only females on the job. I love that it's got this stigma and it's been this man's job and I get to play a part in changing that image of the trades and doing a man's job but doing it even better than they do and looking good doing it.

"I have my nails done and I have my false eyelashes. I get to be girlie, but I work hard."

•

John Burcaw is right: not only have more people stopped looking down their noses at skilled trade work, but more college graduates are reversing course to enter the trades. Eight percent of community college students—or one in twelve—already have a bachelor's degree, according to the American Association of Community Colleges. That's nearly a million students. Some are learning new skills for their jobs, but many have been dissatisfied with where their bachelor's degrees have led them, or not led them, and are entering new, well-paid careers with steady incomes.

Megan Kinch was one of those who went from academia to skilled trade—not because she didn't love her academic pursuits. But she had to make a living, and her college education wasn't getting her there.

Megan, who's lived her whole life in Toronto, was a first-generation college student and the road was never easy. She dropped out for a while and spent some time in the military, then went to university part-time and finally switched to full-time, studying anthropology.

"I had a great educational experience and got into grad school with scholarships," she said. She was revising a paper that was supposed to be published in a book. And then she fell down the stairs and broke her back.

She had finished all her classwork toward her master's degree but was too disabled to complete her thesis. Despite the lower tuition costs in Canada for university, the cost of college was too much, and debt was stacking up. She also needed to take care of her mother, who was sick. Her college work, which was mainly academic rather than practical in nature, "ended up being pretty much useless," she said. "It's a common experience for working-class students."

Megan lived on welfare for a year and spent a couple of years recovering from her injury. Then came the recession of 2008-09.

She was able to get some work as managing editor of a journal and doing work for a nonprofit, work that's difficult to get with organizations that don't have the resources to pay well. Megan made $3,000 to produce an entire magazine. In 2013, she gave birth to a baby girl, but her relationship didn't last, so she also became the single head of a family.

When her daughter was very young, Megan switched to being an electrician.

Though she'd majored in anthropology, she had always excelled at math and wanted to use it. She also chose electronics because, among the skilled trades, it had more women. In this case, "more" meant between 1 percent and 2 percent. In plumbing, by contrast, women made up half of one percent of the workforce.

The YWCA was offering a course in electrical work. Megan left her university education completely off her résumé in order to apply, thinking it might work against her. She did mention that she'd taken a year of physics.

She applied to the union and worked at what she called "horrible nonunion jobs" to convince the union that she had a credible future as an electrician. That was followed by a seven-year apprenticeship, interspersed with training periods of eight weeks at a time.

When I talked with Megan, who is now in her early forties, she had just finished her apprenticeship and had a provisional electrician's license. That gave her one year to pass the electrician's test. She was making $38 an hour, which would go up to $45 after the test. But it's not easy being one of the few women on the job.

"I like the work," she said, "but the conditions are bad. Just no women. No women's bathroom. Or there will be a women's bathroom, but it will be locked. I'm really sick of that."

The work is more fun and exciting than professional office work, she said, which is why she's seeing a lot of people attending university and then changing their minds to enter skilled trades.

"I meet a lot of guys who have a degree and go into accounting. A lot of professional jobs pay really poorly, and a lot of trades are unionized. In a lot of trades, people are paying off student debt [from attending college for professional jobs]. For women, trades is often a second or third career move. Almost every woman I know in trades has a similar story."

Megan's life has since expanded in some new ways. She's been able to do more work in the writing world, even winning a grant and bringing in a significant amount of her income via creative work.

She has no regrets about her university studies. She loved anthropology and would have stayed in it if the financials were workable. But she knows now that if she finds herself unemployed, or if the writing hits a slow period, the union will be able to find her another electrical job. Her parents have since died, but her daughter is in elementary school, and Megan gets necessary stability from knowing she'll be able to support her little family.

At the same time, she's aware that having union membership is also an advantage that many people aren't given. "I want to acknowledge the tremendous privilege that I have as a white person. Had I not been a white person, I wouldn't have had the opportunities I've had." When she was applying at the union, she was one of five female applicants, three of whom were Black. None of the Black applicants were accepted.

PAY IN THE SKILLED TRADES

Here are the average salaries for some of the skilled vocational trades in 2021, according to the US Bureau of Labor Statistics. Keep in mind that union members generally are paid more, as well as skilled workers who own their businesses, and that the range of income can vary widely.

Construction manager: $98,890
Elevator technician: $97,860
Power plant operator: $94,790
Avionics technician: $65,550
Boilermaker: $64,290
Electrician: $60,040
Plumber: $59,880
Drywall finisher: $48,040
Welder: $47,010
(Specialized welder: $100,000+)
Auto mechanic: $46,880
Hair stylist: $38,910

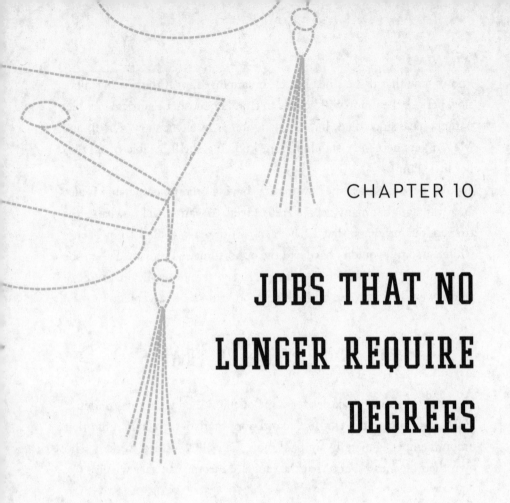

CHAPTER 10

JOBS THAT NO LONGER REQUIRE DEGREES

It's a gift to know from an early age, deep within us, what we absolutely want to do with our lives. And a phenomenal frustration to think that our goal is out of reach.

Justin Mutawassim found the gift when he took his first plane flight, from his home in New York City to Walt Disney World in Florida, a celebration of his fifth birthday.

He peeked his little head in at the flight deck, and the pilot and copilot invited him in (this was pre-9/11). "They said, 'Now don't press any buttons,' and I wanted to press them *all*. What *were* all these things?"

Years later, his mother found a picture he'd drawn back then of himself as a pilot.

A couple of years after the Disney trip, Justin and his mother moved to Texas; his parents had divorced a few years earlier. One thing sure didn't change: his fascination with planes. A flight-simulation game he was given at age twelve became his nonstop passion. A discount coupon his parents found earned him an hour of flight instruction at age sixteen.

Yet the dream seemed frustratingly out of reach. Justin was told by a teacher that someone who wears glasses can't be a pilot. This was outdated information; although flight schools once only accepted students with excellent eyesight, today many commercial and private pilots fly with corrective lenses. But Justin also learned that pilots for major airlines needed to have bachelor's degrees—a requirement that largely stemmed from the military, where most commercial pilots had gotten their start and which required a bachelor's degree for those spots.

For many years, the United States was the only country in the world where major airlines required a bachelor's degree for their pilots. It makes little sense to me. In what way would a bachelor's in, say, philosophy qualify someone to be a pilot more than a certificate or associate's degree in avionics and lots of specific training?

In any case, Justin had neither the money nor the grades for four-year college. Classwork just wasn't his strong point.

Besides, there weren't a lot of role models for him as a Black high school student. Only about 2 percent of pilots for major airlines are Black.

Justin had plenty of other interests in high school, many that revolved around the school's expensive new stadium and auditorium. He took culinary classes to work in food service at the stadium and did videography and radio broadcasting, especially for high school sports.

He figured he'd study communications at the nearby community college so that he could save money living at home, and maybe one day he'd be able to work as an announcer at a sports station like ESPN. It wasn't his dream, but maybe it would be enough.

But the community college was depressing. The hallways were dark, and the atmosphere was grim. His friends were all away at state college. His grades were subpar.

"I said, 'This is not working. Let's just take a break.'"

Nothing appealed to him except planes, so he got a job as a baggage handler just so that he could be around them. He was hired by Delta Airlines, making $9 an hour at age eighteen.

"My parents said, 'You're absolutely crazy,'" Justin recalled. "'With the commute and the tolls, you'll barely be making any money.' And I said, 'Just let me do what I want to do for the first time.'"

He loved it and was promoted within months, overseeing the cleaning and deicing of planes between flights, dealing with audits and security. When planes had to be repositioned, he'd get to be up on the flight deck talking to traffic control. He figured he'd continue to get pay raises and be a happy man. He had no idea.

Justin's coworkers, most of them older than he, urged him to think more ambitiously. The heavy physical labor would take its toll over time. He thought about becoming an air traffic controller, which doesn't require a bachelor's and pays well into the six figures. But then he had a chat with a pilot he'd seen around who went out of his way to be friendly. The pilot gave Justin his number. When Justin failed to call because he was too nervous, the pilot came looking for him.

So many times, listening to the success stories of people without bachelor's degrees, I'm struck by how one kind person can make all the difference. In Justin's case, the pilot "just took the time and talked to me like a human." So let me just take a moment here to say: When you have made it in your field, and you will someday, please take the time to be that one kind person for someone else. When you see how important networks and mentoring have been to your own success, you'll know it all works best when we pull others up with us. Finding our best life is not a zero-sum game.

The pilot gave Justin the number of a Black pilot who knew about flight training in the Dallas area. And that pilot filled him in on the local flight schools and the licenses he'd need to become a pilot. Flying for a small regional airline would not require a degree.

The mentor also helped Justin talk to his mother about the big loan—$90,000—he would need for his training in a fast-track program.

A whole series of written exams had to be completed before the actual flight testing for each skill. Justin was so ardent about his goal that he had already completed six of these written exams before he started flight school. He was twenty years old when he entered school in 2016. And it took him less than a year to get all his licenses.

But that just kicked in the next phase: instrument training and the required fifteen hundred hours of flight time to become an airline pilot. In order to get those hours, he took yet *more* training to become a flight instructor, obtaining eight different licenses in about five months. It was, he said, "the best time of my life."

Justin had a chance to fly in some advanced private jets, and then he got a job out of Indianapolis flying for a regional airline.

"It was an absolute blast," he said. "I got to fly to Canada, got to fly to the Bahamas a little bit."

The pandemic cut into his career for a while. But he made it through, thanks to the strong financial-management skills his accountant mother had instilled in him. After the pandemic, he went to work for another small airline. But this also was a time when labor shortages were hitting many industries, and a lot of commercial pilots were retiring. As their planes took to the skies again, airlines were faced with a scarcity of pilots. In response, many major airlines started dropping their college-degree requirements. Delta, Justin's dream airline, followed suit in January 2022. At age twenty-five, he was hired to fly for the company.

"The walls are falling down in the industry," he said.

At the time we talked in 2023, Justin was flying coast to coast and to countries on four continents. He was making $108,000 a year and looking forward to his one-year anniversary, when his hourly rate would jump to $171. He recently completed his captain's training for the Boeing 757 and 767, making him the youngest Black captain in the company's history, he said, and giving him another major jump in pay for those flights.

The loan his mom took out for him was paid off within a few years, even with COVID-19 disrupting his plans for a while.

"There's nothing wrong with not going to college," Justin said. "There's nothing wrong with not following the societal norms. You might feel lost at the moment, but put yourself out there to give it a try. Think, *Who can I talk to?* You try to network and find mentors who are like-minded."

•

Delta Airlines is one of the most dramatic examples of a company waking up to modern realities and recognizing that it simply doesn't make sense to require a four-year degree for certain kinds of jobs, even when that's been the tradition for decades.

But it's just one of a wave of employers that have dropped the bachelor's degree as a requirement for certain jobs. In 2022, the US Office of Personnel Management told federal agencies to base hiring more on skills than on degrees, except in cases where formal education is required by law. And states are starting to follow suit.

It's happening through big parts of the private sector too, according to a 2022 report by Harvard Business School and Emsi Burning Glass Institute, a think tank on the future of work. These organizations have tracked degree requirements since 2014 and found the following, which by now should come as no surprise to you. It certainly didn't to me:

"Among middle-skilled occupations, the skill requirements of those openings that require degrees are, for the most part, not significantly different from those openings for which no degree is required. Degree requirements seemed to function instead as a proxy used to simplify the hiring process, a shorthand for certain skills and a screen to reduce the number of candidates whom recruiters needed to evaluate."[1]

In other words, employers use degrees as a requirement to make their hiring jobs simpler, not because people without a college degree might not be just as qualified or even more qualified. For any given job, people without degrees are doing the same work as the people who went through a four-year college.

For the 2022 report, the researchers analyzed more than fifty-one million job postings and found that even before the pandemic, "between 2017 and 2019, 46 percent of the middle-skill and 31 percent of the high-skill occupations we studied experienced material declines in degree requirements."

If what we had before was degree inflation, maybe we can call this the start of degree deflation. And it was happening to some extent in nearly two-thirds of occupations, the report said, but especially finance, business management, engineering, and health care.

The job networking site LinkedIn also noticed a switch to skills-based hiring. In a 2022 report, the company said that 40 percent of employers were looking primarily at skills to make their hires—twice as many as the year before.

The tech sector has long been a leader in dropping the bachelor's degree requirement, which makes sense. For one thing, some of its biggest names—Bill Gates of Microsoft, Steve Jobs of Apple, Mark Zuckerberg of Facebook/Meta—never graduated college. And it's clear that digital natives are adept coders who accomplish some remarkable innovations.

There also are tech-based skills that can be taught in far less than four years, or even two.

A lot depends on the individual company. Accenture and IBM were among the first and most committed to dropping degree requirements for many jobs. The 2022 report noted that for jobs as a software quality assurance engineer, only 26 percent of Accenture's postings required a degree, and 29 percent of IBM's. Oracle, Intel, HP, and Apple, on the other hand, required a degree in at least 90 percent of postings for these jobs.

In 2020, Google announced that it was offering several online certificate courses, taught via the platform Coursera, to help launch people without college degrees into white-collar futures in the tech world. The courses cost about $300 each, take five or six months, and cover cybersecurity, data analytics, digital marketing/e-commerce, IT support, project management, and UX design.

The bigger part of the announcement was that Google vowed to make the certificates count as the equivalent of college degrees for people applying to Google in jobs related to their courses. As this book went to press, it was too early to gauge results from the certificate program; the 2022 Harvard/Emsi report showed Google as one of the companies where 90 percent or more of job postings required a college degree.

Apple also has since said that college training is often a mismatch for the skills it seeks—mainly, coding—and that it is hiring more people who aren't graduates. Dell announced an initiative in 2019 to hire more people straight from community colleges.

Corporate certificate courses and lofty announcements by these large companies aside, a lot of the hiring of nondegreed tech people *is* happening, albeit in smaller, more flexible companies. And one of the more popular nonbachelor's pathways to well-paid tech jobs is through so-called coding boot camps: crash courses that last anywhere from a few months to a year. Costing between $10,000 and $20,000, these boot camps are not cheap, but some offer guarantees that if you're not placed in an appropriate job afterward, you don't have to pay the tuition.

Private coding camps work for a lot of people, but be sure to check them out carefully before you sign up. Don't be overly impressed if the name of a prestigious university is attached to a camp; coding camps are generally privately run, and you're not being taught by the university's professors. Make sure courses cover software development, the hot field of cybersecurity, and data analysis. Check out their job-placement services as well, plus any guarantees, and be sure to speak with graduates of the program—and not the graduates the school offers to set you up to meet.

"Not all boot camps are created equal," said Scott Thayer, who made a successful transition from painting houses to coding via a boot camp.

"There are straight scams—a bunch of videos you could have found else-where for less or free. They promise you jobs. Really do the research and ask around on Reddit or other internet forums."

Scott, who hails from Michigan, said that though all his siblings went to college, the idea didn't attract him, and he had no idea what he wanted to study. He figured he'd join the US Army, but during his medical evaluation, he was found to have very flat feet and was rejected. It was 2012, and the Army was having no problem filling its slots; it could afford to be choosy. He tried community college but wasn't attending his classes and failed.

He took an EMT course but realized the job paid poorly and seemed a path to burnout. His mental health was poor, and he saw a high-stress job as problematic. He started working at a restaurant, tried community college again, did better for three semesters, and then realized he simply hated college and didn't want the debt of a four-year degree.

He met friends who, along with a therapist, "pulled me from my annoying mental state." He found work at a tapas restaurant but, after three years of night and weekend work, was frustrated that he was missing out on leisure time with friends and siblings.

He talked to a contractor who had painted the restaurant where he worked and was hired on as a residential painter working at upscale homes. "I really enjoyed it and was learning that craft."

He moved on into making high-end cabinets, working with stains and lacquers. It was interesting and creative work, but he said, "I realized that you end up with your hands destroyed and your lungs destroyed. The money was fine, but the trajectory wasn't there. You have to have your own business in that field if you want to support a family."

And though he liked seeing the work he produced, "I was missing the brain part of it. I really do like learning. I just don't like school."

Scott had gotten married, and his wife is a software developer with a degree in computer science. His father and brother had also worked in that world. "I had played around with coding and enjoyed it and thought, *I think I can do this.*" He met a couple of people who had gone to coding boot camp and both had had great experiences. He and his wife talked about it for several months and decided to make the investment—which also meant her supporting the household.

He chose a full-time camp; many schools also offer a part-time option. It cost about $10,000.

"Right at the beginning, I felt very connected," Scott said. "Partly it was the classmates and instructor coming from different retail and trade jobs. I felt right at home."

He didn't skate through; this was a serious boot camp, and he found some of the concepts challenging. But he made it.

What he thought really made the difference, however, was the career-services arm of the boot camp, which didn't just provide connections but worked on interview and job-hunting skills. Scott was hired as a junior software developer by a small company in Nebraska that had gone from using all in-house employees pre-pandemic to hiring remote workers. Today, about 40 percent of the staff is remote.

It's a great fit for him. "The language and frameworks they were using were the ones I was specializing in at my boot camp," he said. The product team assembles the different features of the software and break those down into smaller tasks that are assigned to the developers. Scott is part of a team taking on those tasks.

Each morning, the entire company of about fifty people jumps on a video call. In addition to work announcements, they celebrate birthdays and anniversaries, welcome new people, and spend time socializing.

When I talked to Scott six months into his job, in 2022, he was earning $60,000, more than he had expected. But better, he saw a trajectory for his future.

"There's always upward momentum," he said. "I'll probably get promoted to midlevel in a couple of years. And I enjoy it. My stress levels are way down."

Learning is part of the attraction. As Scott says, he loves to learn—just not in school.

"I'm just constantly looking things up, whether it's internal documentation or if it's a task I don't quite know what to do with, I have sources I can go to and learn from. The senior developers are very helpful and friendly."

●

Jeff Rigby represents another common scenario for people who work in tech without a bachelor's: he's naturally good at it, he keeps learning, and he does it quickly.

"I never really did well in school," he said. "I never put in the effort. I was always just interested in other things. I didn't have a lot of direction."

Jeff attended Central Connecticut University for a year and described it as "okay." But he landed in tech without even realizing it.

His part-time job from middle school through that year of college was handling the tech side of things for a music store. He picked up more freelance work in tech, and then the owner of the music store introduced him to a man who was starting a business. The man offered him a full-time job after his first year of college, doing web design and programming.

"I did kind of b.s. my way into that job," Jeff said. "One of my skills is being able to pick up on things quickly in tech. And it was just a couple of people, so expectations weren't high for an eighteen-year-old kid. It was all self-directed. I would have to figure out how to accomplish any given task."

He searched online for solutions when he didn't know them; for a while, an accomplished freelancer worked at the business and taught him some of the ropes.

After three or four years, the business wasn't doing that well, so Jeff logged into Monster.com and updated his résumé. He wasn't actively looking for positions, but he was contacted by a New York City company because of his skills in design and page layout. The company did a lot of work on page layout for magazines and newspapers, and his skills matched their particular needs.

"Just, again, super lucky," is how Jeff described it.

He was the first person without a college degree to be hired at the company, he was told. And he stayed six years, learning new skills including Drupal and open-source content management systems. Then he got a call from a recruiter looking for someone with exactly those skills.

"I asked for way more than they offered, and they said yes immediately. That was a pretty big salary jump for me." Jeff is still with the Montreal-based company—it has a New York office—which serves as a sort of liaison between drug companies and doctors. Married and in his early forties, he mostly works from home and earns $190,000 a year.

Despite his success, Jeff has had years of regret about not going to college, not having the same experience that his peers did. It's a shame that our society makes people feel that way; there are many ways of missing out in life. It's important to Jeff that his two children go to college.

What's *not* important to him is hiring only people who went to college.

"I interview a lot of job applicants now, and we never ask where people went to school," Jeff said. "It's more about 'What is your experience, and can you do the job?'"

•

While the tech sector has been at the forefront of degree deflation, it's also well known for its ups and downs. In 2023, many of the large companies that had been on hiring sprees started paying people to leave. That includes Meta, Salesforce, Amazon, Accenture, and Microsoft.

The health-care sector, by contrast, has grown steadily and is projected to continue to expand across the nation, especially in the so-called allied health jobs—in other words, not doctors, dentists, or nurse practitioners—that don't require a bachelor's degree.

According to a 2022 report by the Bureau of Labor Statistics, the health-care and social assistance sector is projected to create the most jobs over the 2021-31 decade, adding about 2.6 million positions.[2]

And significantly for people without a bachelor's degree, the allied health-care occupations, which already make up more than half of jobs in the industry, are projected to grow the fastest during that time.

As in other industries, the retirement of older employees is creating openings. And the stresses of being frontline health-care workers during the pandemic, often under taxing conditions, prompted many to leave the industry.

The health-care field has been especially open to apprenticeships, which have been pitched to hospitals and medical organizations by training companies as a much quicker way to bring on the skilled workers they need. Try doing an internet search for "health-care apprentice" or the specific job you're interested in. Chances are that multiple possibilities will pop up.

More than most, the industry also offers a natural trajectory to better-paying jobs. It's called "stacking." For example, a nursing career can start with a job as a certified nursing assistant, usually working in a nursing home–type setting. It requires only a high school degree and three to eight weeks of training for a certificate. Becoming a licensed practical nurse, who provides primary patient care such as starting an IV and taking blood pressure, requires a year in a nursing program, usually set up so that working people—such as nursing assistants—can attend.

Those who want to move to jobs with greater responsibility and higher pay can study to become a registered nurse. Employers, in need of these nurses, will often pay their way through training. Becoming an RN, which allows nurses to provide patient care in a wide variety of settings, requires an associate's degree, with pay averaging about $75,000 a year. But nurses can earn more if they decide to then go for a bachelor's or even a master's degree—again, with employers frequently willing to pick up the tab. And it can go on from there, all the way to a doctorate.

The great thing here is that you're not committing from the start to an expensive and time-consuming four-year college education. You get to enter the field with a minimum of training and see whether the work suits you, spend time with and learn from the people doing the next level of work, and determine whether that's something you want to do as well. And you usually can work while studying your way to the next level.

Similarly, a sterile processing technician can become a surgical technician.

Keep in mind that there are big differences in how much people are paid in allied health-care careers. Dental hygienists, who need an associate's degree to practice, earn an average of $81,400, while dietetic technicians, with the same education requirements, earn an average of $33,730, according to the Bureau of Labor Statistics.

Within the burgeoning health sector, one of the fastest-growing demands is for physical therapy assistants, the bureau reports. While physical therapists diagnose patients' conditions and prescribe a program of massage, exercise, and other treatments, the assistants are often the ones who carry out those programs and have the most patient contact. As baby boomers age and older bones and muscles develop painful conditions, the need for physical therapy will grow as well.

It's also among the higher-paid support jobs and especially good for people who like working with and encouraging people.

•

Blake Dubbert had found physical therapy an interesting career possibility ever since he was a kid who had been helped through what appeared to be a case of juvenile rheumatoid arthritis, though the diagnosis wasn't entirely clear. The exercises helped him build up strength and reduce pain.

But then he found out that becoming a full-fledged physical therapist would require a doctorate: four years of undergraduate school plus three years of grad school.

"I had to put myself through school, and a doctorate would be prohibitively expensive," Blake said. "The debt-to-earnings ratio for a physical therapist is not stellar."

Blake had no real idea of what he wanted to do in life, and math came easily to him. He decided to become an accountant and did two years at his local community college in Columbia, Tennessee. But he realized accounting wasn't for him; maybe he would become a teacher. He was accepted to a private four-year college in Nashville with a full scholarship, but it was the middle of the academic year, and he couldn't get the financial award unless he started in the fall.

So he started scrolling through the academic offerings at another community college to see what interested him, and an associate's degree in becoming a physical therapy assistant was among the offerings. Learning about the body and kinesiology opened up a new world to him. He was hooked and said good-bye to any thought of getting a bachelor's degree.

It took only two years and about $10,000 to get his degree, books included. Had he decided on the field from the start, it would have cost a lot less; Tennessee provides two years of free community college to state residents.

His career suffered a slowdown because of the pandemic; only absolutely necessary therapy was being offered. But he was able to get a job at a rehab facility that was one of the few nursing homes in the area that accepted COVID-positive patients. He eventually switched over to acute care at a nonprofit hospital in his community, first by working on an on-call basis while he still had the rehab gig and eventually coming on full-time.

The work has a lot of variety. There are stroke patients, heart-attack patients, and people recovering from amputations. He helps determine when patients are ready to leave the hospital and go to rehab. And he gets patients up and moving after surgery, crucial to avoiding postsurgical blood clots.

Now age twenty-six, he's married to a nurse who, as it happens, is working her way up the ladder of nursing levels, with her education paid by the hospital that employs her.

But Blake has no similar ambitions. He still finds that the debt-to-income ratio in his field "makes zero sense" and feels he has better things to do with his young life than study for five more years. His $76,000 income (and that's before overtime pay) is only about 15 percent lower than that of a full physical therapist in his area. Combined with his wife's income, they're living well.

"I very much enjoy my work and get a lot out of it," Blake said. But he also has a lot of outside interests and would like to semi-retire in his early forties to pursue those: exercise, reading, crocheting stuffed animals, and doing outdoorsy things with his wife. The plan is to keep a hand in, do on-call work, achieve a good work-life balance, and bring relief to the people who need the kind of help he needed as a kid.

WHERE DEGREE REQUIREMENTS ARE DROPPING

Here are the jobs that experienced the biggest drops in the requirement for a bachelor's degree from 2017 to 2020, according to a study by the Harvard Business School and Emsi Burning Glass Institute. The first set of jobs experienced structural changes in degree requirements, which means that they were not responding to the pandemic or other changes in the market; these are more likely to be permanent changes, and you can probably expect more employers to drop the requirements for a college degree in those fields. The second group are cyclical, which means they responded to changes in the marketplace. They might or might not continue to lower degree requirements.

Structural

> Health-care administrator—Health Care
> Insurance sales agent—Finance
> Network/Systems administrator—Information Technology
> General manager—Business Management and Operations
> Personal financial adviser—Finance
> Construction manager—Construction, Extraction, and
>   Architecture
> Loan officer—Finance

Office manager—Clerical and Administrative

Computer programmer—Information Technology

Compensation/benefits analyst—Human Resources

Store manager/supervisor—Sales

Real estate agent/broker—Sales

Maintenance supervisor—Maintenance, Repair, Installation

Preschool teacher—Education

Production supervisor—Manufacturing

Coach—Education

Sales supervisor—Sales

Property manager—Business Management and Operations

Bill and account collector—Clerical and Administrative

Human resources assistant—Human Resources

Cyclical

Sales representative—Sales

Recruiter—Human Resources

Software quality-assurance engineer—Information Technology

Labor relations specialist—Human Resources

Database administrator—Information Technology

Clinical case manager—Health Care

Nursing manager—Health Care

Executive assistant—Clerical and Administrative

Customer service manager—Customer and Client Support

Banking branch manager—Finance

Registered nurse—Health Care

Bookkeeper/accounting clerk—Finance

Computer support specialist—Information Technology

Intensive/critical care nurse—Health Care

Sales assistant—Sales

Billing clerk/specialist—Clerical and Administrative

Construction foreman—Construction, Extraction, and
   Architecture

Interpreter/translator—Design, Media, and Writing
Insurance claims—Finance
Residential assistant/adviser—Community and Social Services

HEALTH-CARE SUPPORT JOBS: WHICH ONES PAY?

The demand for skilled employees is increasing in pretty much all of the health-care jobs that don't require a bachelor's degree, but some pay well while others don't provide a living wage. Here, according to the US Bureau of Labor Statistics, are some of the best-paying jobs and some of the worst. Note that most of the well-paid jobs require an associate's degree or another two-year training course; some employers require a bachelor's degree while others don't. These are averages; many employees make more as they add experience and training or depending on the demand and cost of living in their area.

Well Paid

Health-care administrator: $101,340
Registered nurse: $89,010
Nuclear medicine technologist: $85,480
Dental hygienist: $84,440
Ultrasound technologist: $81,290
MRI technologist: $80,100

Low Paid

Physical therapy aide (not assistants): $31,410
Dietetic technician: $33,730
Orderly: $34,510
EMT: $36,330
Psychiatric technician: $37,200
Phlebotomist: $38,460

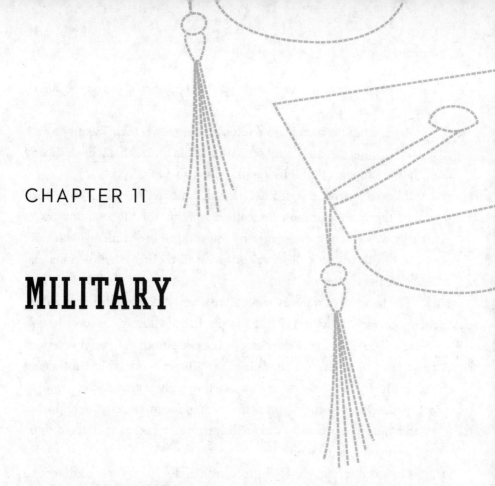

CHAPTER 11

MILITARY

Alixandra Yang's family didn't have money to put her through college.

Ali, the name she goes by, was attending DePaul University in Chicago, planning to major in Spanish and go into foreign service. But she was working four part-time jobs to make it happen, she and her mother had taken out hefty loans, and it was all too much. So she joined the US Navy, where she would serve close to seven years.

Soon after her service ended, she landed a job with a future in Denver that paid $110,000 a year. That was partly a result of the management and administrative skills she learned and practiced during her service. She also took advantage of a job-placement program for veterans. On top of that, she's fluent in Korean, a language she hadn't known before but learned during a year and a half of intensive language school, courtesy of the navy. Plus she was able to finish her college degree with the substantial financial help of the GI Bill, which pays from 40 percent to 100 percent of college costs, depending on the type of college and the length and type of service.

Ali and her husband, also a veteran, are well on their way to providing their young son and daughter with a stable future that includes many of the enrichments that Ali's family wasn't able to afford.

It doesn't surprise you, I bet, that the military has historically been one of the most common noncollege options for high school grads. Usually, school counselors offer two possibilities to students who can't attend or don't want college at this point in their lives: skilled manual trades or the military.

The benefits of military service are many. There can be large enlistment bonuses, and the GI Bill has put many a serviceperson through college. That's how my dentist got his education. As you'll see from the stories here, despite the image of military work as just following orders all day long, people are expected to show a tremendous amount of independence in their work. In a common scenario, they're told what to accomplish, not how to accomplish it, which means they learn to be inventive and determined.

On a military cargo flight to Greenland—I was on assignment to observe research in the fjords—I ended up in conversation with a young woman who was the payload manager for Greenland, meaning she was responsible for ensuring that all the cargo on US military planes was properly loaded and secure, and the passengers safely escorted and in place. What she loved about it most was that Greenland is a tough place to get the work done. Weather can be a bear to work with in the Arctic at the one airport that can take planes that big. There isn't a lot of backup equipment or personnel. So, she said, she gets to—*has* to—do whatever it takes. She loves the challenge and independence.

In the military, you serve your country and in the process can learn about well-paid fields such as cybersecurity, coding, and mechanics. You probably guessed that much. But what you might not have guessed is that you also can be trained in many more unusual occupations. Musical instrument repair? Weather forecasting? Journalism? See the list in this chapter.

The upsides are many, but let's not get too rosy. As you'll see from the stories here, some veterans are happy with their military past and recommend it, while others have mixed or negative feelings. There's the obvious: In many military jobs, you could end up in combat or other perilous assignment. Living conditions are often tightly regimented and less than comfortable.

Beyond that are more commonplace complaints, about long-term physical problems—hearing loss from continual exposure to loud noise comes up a lot—unmet expectations, and unhappiness with certain aspects of military culture, including the treatment of some gay service members. The veterans in this chapter offer advice about what to expect and how to go about planning for your best possible future if you pick the military route.

Despite her efforts at DePaul, Ali had thought about joining the navy "for as long as I could remember." Her great-grandfather had served in World War II. "He used to babysit me and draw little anchors on my knuckles," she said.

While she was struggling financially in school, Ali started a relationship with a student who was in the Marine Corps and was using the GI Bill to afford college. The two would later marry. She also learned that military vets get preferential consideration for government jobs, and her goal at the time was to work for the State Department.

More than one of the branches offered a shot at learning and working with foreign languages. But the navy stood out: it would give her $65,000 in student-loan repayments for the loans she and her mother had already taken out. "And I said, hey, yeah!"

Ali became fluent in Korean during her year and a half of language training, and then took an assignment as the executive assistant to the number-two naval officer in South Korea. There, she did a little translating and interpretation, writing reports and so forth, among other duties. Then she was transferred to Hawaii, where she was put in command of the language office. That might sound like just the job for a woman with her background, but the work was administrative rather than linguistic. Ali was in charge of training for all the sailors in the command, making sure they were properly tested. She moved up into management, responsible for sixty-five people. But it wasn't the work she'd been expecting and looking forward to as a newly minted Korean speaker and writer: "I was a one-person HR department," she said. One bright spot: she was able to finish her college education while still in the navy.

Toward the end of her service, Ali could have gone back to South Korea, but her husband didn't speak the language. By this time, she was no longer interested in State Department work; she wanted the freedom to travel where she wanted and when. And she wanted stability for the family she and her husband were starting.

She heard about Hiring Our Heroes, a group that helps place veterans in apprenticeships at companies and organizations. Ali was able to snare an internship at tech company VMWare in the Denver area, and she felt happy and supported in the culture there. That led to a permanent job as an account manager.

Things worked out well in the end for Ali, but that doesn't make her a big advocate of joining the military. Her husband, who was in the infantry, has lasting injuries from training accidents and underwent a lot of "general wear and tear" from carrying gear as well as hearing loss from being around firearms his entire time in the military.

While Ali's desk job was less physically demanding than her husband's, being on call 24/7 was exhausting. The pressure was always on. "We often were told that our work could be life or death for our shipmates in the fleet, so that constant pressure takes a toll on mental health," she said. Also, there was continual testing for both promotion and keeping up language skills. One bad grade would cause a panic that she might not hold on to her job.

For those who feel that the many benefits of military life outweigh the potential stresses, Ali and the other military veterans suggest checking out *all* the branches carefully to see what they offer. She says that the navy and air force are generally the better fit if you know from the start what career path you want. Some will commit to that path for you before you enlist (though Ali's ability to use her Korean at work didn't last very long). Look at each offering that interests you carefully to find out the time commitments involved and where you are likely to be stationed— though no one can make guarantees. Conditions can change in the world and on the political front in unforeseeable ways. You have to work where and how the military wants you to, no matter what you signed up to do.

Still, recruiters are hungry for enlistees, Ali said, so ask for what you really want and make decisions based on their offers. "They need you more than you need them," she said. Find out what kind of signing incentives are offered and whether you're guaranteed the kind of training you want, as well as how much travel is involved and whether you might be in combat situations if there is a conflict.

•

Matthew Bell has no regrets about his four years in the US Marine Corps, though he couldn't have foreseen that where it would lead him was . . . beer.

College was never on Matthew's mind while growing up in Houston. He started working part-time during high school at a Blockbuster Video (remember those?) and simply kept on doing it full-time after graduation. He was promoted and then asked if he wanted to be promoted again. Suddenly he saw his career looking like a long, narrow tunnel. "I took a look at my life and asked, 'Is this really where I want my life to be headed, managing a video store?'" he said. "The answer was no."

Matthew wasn't sure exactly where he did want his life to go long-term. But at least the military would open more options. He chose the marines, in part because he liked the straightforward, no-nonsense demeanor of the recruiter.

Matthew wanted to do something that was based in science and math, so he chose to work in artillery direction and control. It requires tremendous precision to determine which way weaponry will land, taking into consideration such factors as terrain, wind, moisture, and elevation. "There's a lot of book reading and technology," he said. It would put him near the action, he figured, but not in the line of fire. "And I loved it. I really enjoyed it. It was a great experience for me, and I met a lot of great people."

But the military would lead Matthew to a completely different career. Not because of what he did while in uniform, but because of how he spent his spare time while stationed in the San Diego area: he went out with buddies to microbreweries.

"San Diego and Southern California in general has a really wonderful beer scene," Matthew said. He and a friend would visit breweries and brew pubs and, while drinking, listen to the stories of the people who worked in the industry. Many who started up breweries were engineers or scientists or from other interesting walks of life. "I thought, *Wow, I wonder if I can make a career out of this*." He was drawn in by how similar beer making was to his artillery job—the very careful measurement and balancing of countless different factors.

After his four-year tour of duty, Matthew reached out to anyone he could find who was already in the beer industry. He got turned down three times for jobs he really wanted with Flood Independent Distribution, a wholesale craft-beer distributor in Texas. He went to work for another company, but after just a few months there, Flood contacted him and said they'd made a mistake and wanted him to work for them. Now in his late thirties, Matthew has been with Flood for close to a decade, first in San Antonio and now in Houston.

He started as a salesman but worked his way up to middle management, getting the company's products on the shelves of big chain stores throughout Texas. In addition to mastering the logistics of moving product from warehouses to retail in the amounts and at the times they're expected, building relationships is a big part of his work. He earns about $50,000 a year. And the military helped him in more ways than simply exposing him to a world of micropubs.

"There are things about the military that definitely help you become more marketable and disciplined in jobs that require less oversight, which is what you need for sales," Matthew said. "They give you some tools and then unleash you upon the world. They're not going to tell you how to get it done. You have to figure that out, create the plan, and carry out the plan. And you have to manage not just your time but your resources. It's learning project-management skills."

The military was also a place where he built enduring friendships. "I was just asked to be groomsman for a friend I haven't seen for eleven or twelve years," Matthew said. "Those are a lot of really long-lasting relationships."

•

People tend to talk about the military as if it is just one giant organization. And that's true, at least to the extent that almost all of the branches fall within the US Department of Defense. But there are five—or depending on how you count them, possibly six—branches. The choice of which branch to join is at least as important as deciding that you want a future defending your country.

When high school students hear about the military, they tend to think of the US Army. Makes sense: it's the oldest branch (by a few months, anyway) and the largest, with more than 475,000 members. Its image— soldiers fighting on the ground—is the one most familiar from movies.

But every branch has its own areas of specialization and its own benefits and downsides, and within each branch is a dizzying range of opportunities and duties. No matter which branch interests you, be sure to gather all the information, compare offers, and read the contract carefully. Will going into a certain field extend your required service for longer than you find acceptable? If you're promised a certain kind of training, is it spelled out in the contract? Is your enlistment bonus spelled out as well?

When it comes to choosing a branch, here are some preliminary considerations:

Signing bonuses can add up to a hefty $50,000 or more. If this is important to you, check out which branch is offering the best bonuses and for what. There often are add-on bonuses if you sign up for extra years (but keep in mind that you should also ask what kind of reenlistment bonus is offered; it could be that you'd be just as well off with a shorter term and then reenlist if you find you like the military) or can report for duty earlier. Bonuses can change by the year, so don't go by what you see online; ask a recruiter for the latest information. In addition, if you have more than a high school diploma, such as some community-college credits or certificates, you might be able to negotiate higher pay on top of your bonus.

The air force is known as a particularly friendly branch for families and women. Women make up 21 percent of its personnel, compared with about 13 percent for the army and navy. It's also a place where tech-savvy people can work with the latest equipment and train for jobs that translate particularly well into careers after service.

The air force is known for having the best housing, services, and recreation, and in general, its personnel are at somewhat lesser risk of being in active combat than other branches, except for the Coast Guard. The physical fitness requirements are more relaxed as well. But it's also one of the toughest branches to join, in part because of all the perks.

In contrast, the Marine Corps is known for the physical demands it makes of its enlistees. This branch has the toughest basic training and marksmanship course. It's for people who like being outdoors and active. Only about 7 percent of marines are female, a statistic worth investigating further if you're a woman considering this branch.

As an expeditionary force with the capability of deploying anywhere in the world within twenty-four hours, marines are the first responders to sudden military needs, whether it's combat or disaster-relief missions to places suffering a cataclysmic event such as a devastating earthquake. That raises the chances of facing a combat situation.

The army offers the widest selection of jobs. The size of the army provides more opportunity for advancement for those who might be interested in making a career of military work. It also has so many bases around the world that there are more opportunities for families to join army personnel wherever they are deployed. If you're a lover of the coast—and more than half of Americans live within fifty miles of an ocean—the army may not be for you. Most of its bases are inland. It's also a branch in which, if the country does go to war, the chances of seeing combat are high.

Though most of the branches offer opportunity for travel, the navy is particularly famous for it. Long periods at sea are often punctuated by stops at multiple ports and the opportunity to see different places and meet the locals. In fact, if you're a homebody, the navy probably isn't for you. Deployments typically last from six to nine months and can be extended from there. In addition, the training to prepare for deployment is done on board, adding more time. This also makes the navy one of the less-attractive options for families. But its wide range of interesting training opportunities will help lead to jobs afterward.

The Coast Guard is another animal altogether. It's much smaller than the other branches and the only branch that reports to the Department of Homeland Security instead of the Defense Department, because it has both military and civilian duties. Its equipment and staff are permanently stationed in communities, so the likelihood of traveling internationally is low. And even though it is the branch least likely to see combat, the Coast Guard was among the forces getting troops to shore on D-Day.

You're probably most familiar with the Coast Guard's rescue missions at sea, its aid of boaters and ship crews who find themselves in sudden peril. Other duties include drug interdiction, stopping suspected smugglers of undocumented immigrants, helping with cleanup and protection of waters after oil spills, and monitoring the marine environment. And for one Coast Guard veteran, it has led to a path of environmental work that he never would have foreseen.

•

Benjamin Colbert is candid about the forks and detours that map his career. "I'm a case study for why not everybody should go [to college] at eighteen," he jokes.

Now completing a PhD in Environmental Science and Policy, Ben credits his current success to his eight-year tenure in the US Coast Guard. Without it, he probably wouldn't have discovered his passion for marine biology or his aptitude for the rigors of scientific research.

Ben enrolled in Virginia Commonwealth University out of high school but found he lacked direction and wasn't engaged by his courses. Active duty presented itself to Ben as a "soft landing pad," a fluid transition to a new beginning. He'd already enlisted in the Coast Guard Reserve just after high school, with no particular endgame in mind (his father was a reservist). It was a low-commitment (once a month) way to get money to pay for school. Why not? Ben spent the summer before his freshman year of college completing boot camp, and a year later, he enrolled in active duty for a months-long stint. It suited him so well he applied for permanent enlistment.

For enlistees who don't yet have a life's direction in mind, the Coast Guard offers a kind of respite period. All newly enlisted start out as "non-rates," or nonspecialized personnel, and perform general labor while getting acquainted with the various roles available through the USCG. Ben ultimately chose Marine Science Technician "A" School, a nine-week intensive program that teaches about basic pollution investigation and response.

According to Ben, a marine science technician is essentially a regulatory specialist. After training, he became an inspector: someone who audits marine facilities and vessels to enforce federal antipollution regulations.

The work involved some heavy responsibilities. "As a twenty-three- or twenty-four-year old E-4, which is fairly junior, it was often just me and one other person in a car, driving to New York City to be the federal representative for an examination of a large oil-transfer facility, which is a fairly big responsibility. Or I was leading antiterrorism inspections on vessels in New York."

There were disillusioning times as well. "It never feels good to write a $100 ticket for pollution to a multimillion-dollar corporation," Ben said. "It doesn't always feel like you're saving the world."

"But," he was quick to add, "you have the ability within the Coast Guard, especially in the marine science field, to develop competencies and get good at your job in a way that can be rewarding."

His antiterrorism work in the USCG sparked an interest in federal law enforcement. He even completed a bachelor's in organizational leadership to prepare him for future advancement in such a role. Ben asked his superiors to assign him to the Vessel Board and Search Team (VBST), but no open spots were available. He was instead assigned to Waterways Management, a branch that provides services to mariners and issues permits for events on the water. It was comparatively quiet work, Ben was told, which could afford him some downtime, during which he could do work for the VBST. Once he got started at his new post with Waterways Management in Miami, however, he was pleasantly surprised by how much the work agreed with him. South Florida's waters teem with coral reefs, manatees, and seagrass, and Ben got to dive deep into environmental policy and impact analyses. He learned that anytime he issued a permit, it was his job to ensure the permit recipient was compliant with all federal environmental regulations. Working with Waterways Management changed his outlook on the work he wanted to do for the USCG, it changed his career prospects, and ultimately it changed his life.

Ben had always known that the Coast Guard was not going to be his lifelong career. He made the decision to leave the Coast Guard as his ten-year mark loomed on the horizon. He and his wife were expecting their first child and were stationed fourteen hours away from their closest relatives. But he credits his service with helping him land a civilian job with the Department of Defense working in marine resources policy.

He believes that getting a degree is important both for enrichment and to show that you are capable of finishing what you start. But he found his way to a meaningful degree by taking the time to experience life and find studies that would engage him. He eventually earned a master's degree in environmental science and policy and, in 2023, was working toward his PhD—all covered by the GI Bill. His research explores fish hearing and vocalizations and the effects of underwater sound on fishes. Fish can apparently "talk to each other," and disruptions to that, such as from passing vessels, can interfere.

Ben made a point of following up with this caveat: "The military can be very difficult for women. It can be very difficult for people who aren't healthy, straight white males. I am fully recognizing that buried in there is an immense amount of privilege . . . that I am born into, that not everybody has."

·

Given the cautions voiced by some veterans, it's worth examining carefully whether the military is right for you—and under what conditions.

One tiny example: the army will reduce its required active duty from four years to two years for certain kinds of jobs (though reserve duty then is increased). One of these jobs is paralegals, which means that you would receive ten weeks of training to qualify for a job that usually requires a college degree and pays up to six figures. During your tour of duty as a paralegal, there's very little chance you would be placed in a physically dangerous situation.

Or you could be a boots-on-the-ground soldier who has to serve the full four active-duty years, is called into combat, and receives no training that transfers to a job in the outside world, except that many employers have vowed to give hiring preference to veterans. Overall, the unemployment rate for veterans was slightly lower in early 2023 than for the population as a whole (a huge improvement over where it had been in the mid-2010s) but that doesn't mean all groups in the military were equally likely to be employed or in good jobs.

Though top-level officials have tried to knock down some of the racism, sexism, and homophobia that plagued the military, all of those still exist, according to surveys of military personnel, a 2021 investigation by the Associated Press, and many other sources. A survey of Black military members found that a third had experienced racial discrimination, harassment, or both over a single year—and often didn't report the incidents because of lack of confidence in the complaint process.[1]

Physical fitness almost always has to be important to you because you don't have a choice. That's great for some people and not so great for others. There is always the possibility that you could be called into situations in which you could be killed—or be required to kill someone else. You'll likely face long periods of time when you are far from home, family, and longtime friends, though many veterans say the friends made during their days of service are the best buddies they'll ever have. It can be a great fit for people who love the adventure of being off in the world, in completely different surroundings.

Many members of the armed forces say they made their commitments based on whether they liked the attitude of the recruiter or what the recruiter said. But think about it: Would you buy a car based solely on what the salesman said? You need to do objective research, consult people who are in or have served in your branch, in similar roles, and you should fully understand your legal rights, or lack of them. Most veterans I've met say the military honored its side of the enlistment agreement, at least when it came to the training they received—but the agreement is far more binding on *you* than on the military.

You also need to consider what kinds of living conditions work for you, whether you're the type of thinker who finds it hard to accept orders unquestioningly, and how important privacy is to you. You've probably seen classmates in school wracking their brains about every little detail of applying to colleges; you'll need to do just as much work—or even more—to find out whether the tremendous benefits of military service are worth the potential downsides.

•

James Willcox echoes some of Ben's concerns about military life even though he was able to turn the skills he learned in the navy into a lucrative career. In his midthirties, he's earning $150,000 a year.

Originally from a town of five hundred people, about seventy-five miles from New York City, James comes from a family that didn't have enough money to send him to college. He figured military service would give him the needed financial boost into higher education and joined the navy right after high school. He chose it over the army because it allowed him to choose his job from the start: electronics technician, working on, among other things, over-the-horizon radar, which bounces waves off the ionosphere to make radar visible past the horizon.

His four-year stint was enough for him, though. "I didn't want to make the military a career," James said. "I wanted to develop myself."

Still, James is grateful for the aspects of military service that helped launch his career. His work encouraged him to learn about the technical side of operations. And he also had to learn to be organized. "You are very independent in the navy," he said. "You try everything you can before you pull other people in." He was drilled in the understanding that if he didn't do his work right, he was keeping others from doing what they needed to do. It gave him a great sense of responsibility. "It puts a lot of pressure on you, and they encourage people to get down on you if you fail."

That's part of why James thinks some people may not be a good fit for the military. He believes that the pressure can be damaging to people with unresolved issues and advises seeing a therapist before joining. And he would steer anyone away from the military who is easily molded by others.

He was especially disturbed by the way gay men were treated. At the same time, his own thinking about sexuality broadened. James had been raised in a religious Christian family—both his parents are ordained ministers—that frowned on homosexuality. But James made friends in the navy with men who were gay, though he didn't know it for a long time because they were afraid to reveal it.

"A lot of people didn't come out [as gay]," he said. "The few who did had significantly bad stuff happen to them. At night they held a person down by his blankets and literally beat him."

James said physical injury from military duty is another potential issue, not necessarily from combat or abuse but from working conditions. His work often took him to aircraft carriers and other situations where crews weren't provided with adequate ear protection, and the noise was literally deafening—there were times he couldn't hear anything for a half hour after the work ended. He still has mild tinnitus (ringing in the ears) and trouble hearing sounds at certain frequencies.

After his service ended, James was all set to go to college, exactly as he'd planned, with the support of the GI Bill. But he was offered a job in sales with Verizon that paid $55,000. He was in his very early twenties at the time, and that was good pay. He decided he could do without college.

The organization, discipline, and technical skills he'd learned in the navy helped him work his way up in Verizon to the point that within twelve years, he was managing a team of up to thirty-six people who sell to businesses and find solutions for their communication issues. He lives in Chicago on his very comfortable six-figure salary. He's certainly a long way from his modest beginnings in a town where, he says, "the cows outnumbered the people."

TEN INTERESTING JOBS IN THE MILITARY

You probably already have an idea of some of the jobs you could have in the military with or without a degree. And you for sure know about the GI Bill and how it can treat you to up to 100 percent of the cost of going to college. But here are some interesting jobs in the military that might not have occurred to you. They're open to high school grads and translate easily into civilian careers after your stint in the service:

1. *Dog handler.* You'll learn how to train dogs not just in the basics but in highly specialized tasks, such as bomb sniffing, search and

tracking, as well as watchdog work. Civilian dog trainers make up to $100,000 a year, and you would be among the most highly trained. Available in almost all of the armed forces.

2. *Linguist.* Fluency in some languages is a major plus in the outside career world, and in the military, you can learn fluency in a new language in an intensive program that lasts from about nine months to a year and a half. Included are Arabic, Chinese, French, German, Japanese, Portuguese, Russian, and Spanish. You would provide interpretation and translation services during military service. Linguists also might work in cryptology, the coding and decoding of messages. Available in almost all of the armed forces.

3. *Scuba diver and rescue swimmer.* Professional divers in the civilian world work in wide-ranging fields. Scientific diving is needed in archaeology, meteorology, geology, and marine biology. Commercial divers operate underwater heavy equipment for the oil and gas industries and do underwater construction. Underwater welders earn six-figure salaries. Divers also work in the fishery and tourism industries. The top-level jobs, such as saturation divers, who stay underwater for weeks at a time in a pressurized chamber, pay up to about $200,000 a year, depending on how many dives you do. Training to be a professional-level diver is available mainly in the Coast Guard and navy.

4. *Journalist.* In the civilian world, you usually need a bachelor's to get a start in journalism. But if you can pull together compelling sentences—and quickly—and love to tell a good story, you can train as a military journalist writing for news and feature publications in each service. That gives you experience to put on your résumé for jobs after military service. Journalists' pay varies widely from about $40,000 a year to a little more than $100,000. Available in most of the services.

5. *Weather forecaster.* You get to play with all the latest technology to analyze weather patterns and make forecasts for both general

weather and open-water conditions. Full meteorologists study broader weather-related issues, such as climate change. But actual day-to-day forecasting is usually done by weather specialists, often called operational meteorologists. This can lead to several kinds of jobs after the military, including forecasting for TV and radio, that earn up to about $100,000 a year. These are particularly important jobs to the navy and Coast Guard.

6. *Water-treatment specialist and food-safety inspector.* Specialists work to ensure the quality of water in rivers and other bodies of water, especially after troops have finished operations there that might have tainted the water. The specialists analyze water quality, purify and reclaim drinking water when needed, and might operate water-treatment plants on military bases. In the army, they travel with troops and don't just ensure the safety of their water but also teach people in regions without access to clean water how to treat their water to prevent waterborne illnesses that can disable or kill. Water-quality technicians are in huge demand in civilian life at water-treatment plants and other water-quality operations. In the outside world, these jobs generally pay from $50,000 to $85,000 a year. Water-quality specialists are also often trained as food-safety inspectors, who ensure that the food being transported and served in the military is wholesome; as civilians, such inspectors make from $40,000 to $85,000 a year. Both the army and navy offer this.

7. *Musician and instrument repairer.* All the armed forces have bands and seek good musicians, though the opportunities are extremely limited in the Coast Guard. Obviously, you're not going to join the military with no musical background and learn to become a Miles Davis from scratch. But you will receive training and direction to grow your skills. There also are opportunities to write and arrange original music, with training in music theory and individual and group instrumental techniques. You'll leave the military with a résumé that includes performing around the world and

perhaps having your own music performed. The Marine Corps has a special category for musicians: repair techs, who work on restoring and maintaining all kinds of band instruments and receive the training to do that.

8. *Culinary specialist.* You can start your future in cooking and pastry making in any branch of the military. You'll learn a range of cooking skills and a fair amount about nutrition; in addition, you'll put on banquets and other events and be in charge of the business end of purchasing the right amount of food and overseeing the safety of the food you cook. This training prepares you for work not just as a chef or baker but as a caterer or managing a food service or restaurant chain.

9. *Financial management and logistics specialists.* Don't overlook the business operations of the military. It can be a terrific training ground for jobs in banking and other aspects of the financial world. Working as a logistics specialist, you learn about purchasing and the efficient transport of equipment, food, and other items. That's a key component of the manufacturing and retail worlds and what many well-paid mid-level managers do for a living. The world of finance can be difficult to understand, which is why the people who do get it are in high demand. You won't become a wolf of Wall Street through the financial specialist jobs in the military—though you could certainly get there with experience and study afterward. What you will get is a solid grounding in accounting, banking, auditing, and budgeting that can lead to many jobs in civilian life. Financial advisers do not need a college degree. Your grounding in this work in the military, plus some additional study afterward and possibly a certificate course or two, would qualify you for that work, which pays up to $100,000 a year and sometimes more. You'd certainly be a welcome addition to many companies' business-operations offices.

10. *Photographer and videographer.* You'll get training in all aspects of photography including framing shots, printing, and reproduction.

You'll also learn filmmaking and sound technician work, producing everything from still photos for public relations to your own short documentaries on all aspects of military life. It often includes a lot of travel, and you could be stationed on ships or in the air. If the nation is in an armed conflict, it might well mean working in combat conditions. The skills translate to journalism, including television and online video, to filmmaking and general photography. Offered in most branches of the military.

MILITARY BRANCHES

The United States now has six branches of the military—the most recent was added in 2019—ranging in size from about 8,000 active-duty personnel to more than 470,000.

Army

Size: More than 470,000
Established: June 1775
Motto: This We'll Defend
Role: Sustained land combat; border security; international peacekeeping; humanitarian missions.

Navy

Size: More than 343,000
Established: October 1775
Motto: No official motto
Role: Fights wars on the waters and operates submarines and aircraft carriers. Its pilots engage in aerial combat and fly transport and cargo aircraft.

Air Force

Size: More than 328,000

Established: September 1947 (previously part of the Army)

Motto: Aim High . . . Fly-Fight-Win

Role: Defending the skies through aerial combat. It also conducts intelligence, surveillance, and reconnaissance missions.

Marines

Size: More than 170,000

Established: November 1775

Motto: *Semper Fidelis* (Always Faithful)

Role: As an expeditionary force that can fight on land, sea, and air, marines can be moved quickly as the initial fighting force anywhere in the world. They also are a quick-response force in disaster areas, such as after the devastating 2021 earthquake in Haiti, and are the protectors of US embassies and consulates abroad.

Coast Guard

Size: About 35,000

Established: August 1790

Motto: *Semper Paratus* (Always Ready)

Role: Drug interdiction; enforcement of immigration laws; marine environmental protection; rescue of boaters and ship crews in peril.

Space Force

Size: Close to 9,000

Established: December 2019

Motto: *Semper Supra* (Always Above)

Role: The former Air Force Space Command, established as a sixth branch of the military in 2019 (though it remains under the Department of the Air Force), oversees military satellite communications, spaceplanes, the US missile warning systems, and other operations in space.

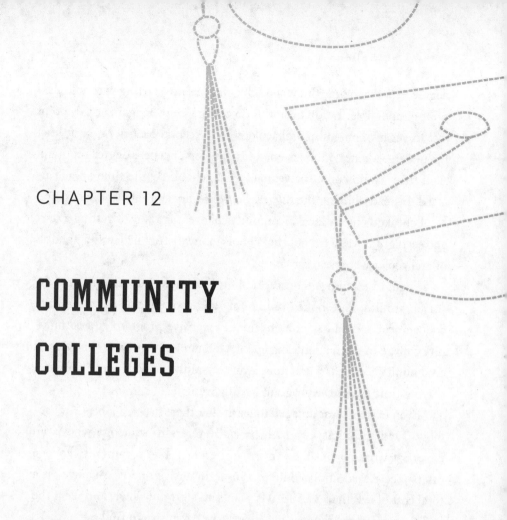

CHAPTER 12

COMMUNITY COLLEGES

Now that I've decided to take a step back from my many years of being a full-time newspaper journalist, I want to go back to something that's fascinated me ever since I was a teenager: archaeology. I've volunteered on a few digs, attended talks, and subscribed to magazines. It's been my own little side passion, and I'm close to ready to spend some real time on it. I've already taken my first course and walk out of each class more excited than I've been in years. (Worth noting: I am better able to engage in the class and understand the material—as well as what the work of an archaeologist entails—because of the years I have spent visiting, reading about, and volunteering at archaeological sites.)

Several years ago, I considered switching careers and pursuing a degree in archaeology. But when I dug deeper into starting over, it looked pretty impossible. I didn't want to do college all over again at this point just to get my courses in archaeology for a second bachelor's, or at least the undergraduate courses needed to apply for a master's degree program. And then would come the years of grad school. By the time I was finished, instead of being the digger, I'd be the ancient relic being dug up.

I checked out my local community colleges, as a way of getting a start and seeing if it was a fit, but the schools in my district had only a handful of archaeology courses, if that.

Then, in the process of researching this book, I decided to turn my search around, and looked online for "archaeology classes community college near me." That brought up an extensive program at a community college in the neighboring county, about one hour away. The closest community college is a half hour away; certainly, I could handle the extra driving time to get the program I really wanted.

Even better, I was amazed to learn that there's such a job as "archaeology field technician," which basically refers to someone who is an expert at working on digs—my favorite part. The community college offers a certificate to become one in an intensive one-year course, at a total cost of less than $1,500. My plan is to start out slowly and see if the reality matches my fantasy, but it won't be expensive to find out.

While most four-year colleges have been slow to change with the times, community colleges have become an ever-better option for people who don't want a four-year degree and can't afford the expense but need some extra education and training to follow their dreams.

For a long time, these colleges, which used to be called junior colleges, mainly awarded two-year associate's degrees, a less expensive and more flexible path to entering a four-year university. They have trained nurses for the first rungs of that career, as well as firefighters, paramedics, dental hygienists, electricians, daycare workers—a whole range of jobs necessary for the functioning of our society and the health and well-being of its people.

But that tells only a fraction of what you can get from community colleges these days. They have become centers of professional certificates and degrees for entering a wide range of fields including some you probably never imagined, like gaming design. And if one day you want to get a four-year degree, you'll be part of the way there. In California, some of them even offer bachelor's degrees, but in an extremely limited number of fields.

•

Christopher Khuong was teaching college courses before he had a bachelor's degree himself.

Born and raised in Houston, Christopher felt lost in high school when it came to applying to colleges. School counselors gave him little guidance on the possibilities, how to apply, or even how to get financial aid. As an artist who was interested in graphic design, he found that counselors spoke mostly about going to art schools. He'd been raised by a single mom who was always working just to support her kids financially; she had neither the time nor the know-how to help with the college application process.

Then a friend said, "Do you know there's a school that teaches gaming design?" Christopher wasn't much into gaming at the time, but the challenges of game design intrigued him. So he applied to that school: Houston Community College. Its costs are low—less than $4,000 a year even now, many years after Christopher got his associate's degree—and it offers open enrollment. And a degree takes only two years.

The number and type of programs at Houston Community College are dizzying. Also available are shorter-term certificates, which generally take far less time to earn than an associate's degree. At HCC, you can be certified in interior design, welding (in hot demand and paying well into six figures for some jobs), cooking and pastry baking, hotel and restaurant management, medical biotechnology (preparing students for roles in research or creating new therapies), filmmaking, fashion design, and a long list of others.

Christopher could have gone the certificate route, but he went for an associate's degree in game design instead, specializing in the artistic end. An art professor mentored him and submitted Christopher's artwork to a competition, which he won—along with some cash. He describes himself as "severely introverted," and this art professor encouraged him to reach higher. "She helped me out and she pushed me to be more—just more. Better at your craft or whatever it is you do."

Mentors have played an important role in Christopher's life.

After getting his degree, Christopher did freelance artwork and graphic design. But then another mentor of his, one of the instructors in the gaming-design department, left to take a job in the industry. Christopher applied for the open instructor job and got it.

Christopher says he'd never thought of going into teaching but found it a natural fit. Even when he was a student, he would tutor others in his classes. And it didn't bother the college that he didn't have a bachelor's (much less an advanced) degree. The school cares more about people's experience and skills than degrees, he said.

After several years of teaching, Christopher entered the University of Houston to get his bachelor's degree in art. It took him four years of part-time attendance to complete; during that time, he continued working full-time. He admits that he didn't need a bachelor's degree. "It was more a matter of pride," he said.

It's not just young people out of high school who benefit from the community college's programs. One of Christopher's students was a security guard who wanted to make video games. After finishing the program, the man was earning enough money in gaming design to buy his grown son a house and truck.

Now in his late thirties, Christopher earns more than $70,000 a year as program coordinator for digital gaming and simulation at Houston Community College, and he loves his work. He's married and was able to buy a house. He doesn't just teach; he's interested in upgrading his own skills with advanced work in 3D design and animation, using the latest software, and does some freelance design work on the side.

The skills involved extend far beyond gaming, he said. One instructor in his program is working with Apple to create ways of teaching people coding and Apple machinery. A company in Ireland that contacted the college is interested in using virtual reality to develop a curriculum for training its employees so that they can "walk" around a virtual engineering room to work with the machinery in a safe environment.

His advice? Don't be afraid of screwing up sometimes. "It's okay to make mistakes as long as you learn from it and have fun," he said. "The learning, it's never over."

•

Community colleges aren't like universities, which offer courses in a broad range of fields. Some community colleges have extensive academics aimed at launching students to four-year schools; others know that many students want skills that are immediately useful in the bigger world.

That's why Pima Community College in Tucson, Arizona, has developed what it calls PimaFastTrack, to give students work-ready skills in weeks rather than semesters or years. The school works with employers in the area to develop programs that provide the maximum chance at a well-paid job with the minimum amount of time invested in education. Started in October 2021, PimaFastTrack "micro-certifications" can be completed in twelve to twenty-four weeks, costing a few thousand dollars rather than tens of thousands of dollars, and are very specific about what they teach. Among the certificates students can earn are project management, accounting, health information systems, and automotive and industrial technology.

The community college is among the relatively few nationwide that have been building white-collar apprenticeships with local industry, especially in the hot field of cybersecurity, said Ian Roark, vice chancellor of workforce development and innovation. And its welding program is extensive; it's expanding from twenty-seven welding booths to forty-three.

Perhaps its most unusual program, though, is in aviation mechanics and avionics technology, or the electronics of air travel including communications and navigation. There are several aviation companies nearby, ready to snap up students who finish degrees and certificates. The college has a large hangar with a 727 donated by FedEx for its students' practical work, and it now has a hangar big enough to hold a 737.

In addition to the aerospace and defense industries in Arizona and Southern California, the college is located near several large aircraft maintenance and repair companies such as Bombardier and Mitsubishi. Those companies have been so eager to hire trained people that the school developed a program in which students could earn FAA avionics credentials within nineteen months. With a few more months of general education, those students could also attain an associate's degree, but the job offers are so fast and so good, Roark said, that few take advantage of it. Starting salaries begin in the $50,000 and above range, Roark said, but depending on the market, it's common for salaries to range up to the six figures.

All community colleges are public and low-cost (not true of all two-year schools, which can be private and costly). But because their offerings can vary widely from one school to the next, it can be a little overwhelming to find just the right school and program. Some areas of study are common to most community colleges—nursing, for example, and business, even entrepreneurship. But if you're interested in a more specific field (such as gaming design for Christopher), do a search for that field along with the phrase "community college." If you need to stay local, add the words "near me." If you can afford to live out of town for a little while, consider it a worthwhile investment. You can almost always mix your studies with working on the outside to help pay the bills.

Work as a social media influencer is a rapidly growing field, commonly bringing in six-figure incomes. Owens Community College in Ohio offers a short-term program in becoming an influencer, in which people are essentially entrepreneurs working their own hours and talking about their own interests, or putting on skits or performances. The industry of social media influencing was estimated at about $21 billion in 2023 and was projected to grow by 30 percent for the next several years.

The list of highly specialized fields of study goes on:

You can learn to make prosthetics at Spokane Falls Community College in Washington State.

Like horses? At Mesalands Community College in New Mexico, you can learn to become a farrier: a specialized blacksmith who makes horseshoes and tends to horses' hooves. The income for farriers has skyrocketed over the past decade and crossed the threshold into six figures in 2017. Farriers in the racing and horse-show industries are particularly well paid, making close to $200,000 annually.

The College of the Florida Keys is located on an island (with very affordable waterfront student residences) and offers degrees and certificates in all sorts of specialized underwater diving, marine science, and seamanship programs. It's also tiny, with fewer than nine hundred students, so there's a real sense of community and personal attention.

Arizona's Pima Community College trains students in solar energy technology, and Mesalands gets them started in wind energy.

Bucks County Community College in Pennsylvania offers an associate's degree in beermaking.

Anne Arundel Community College in Maryland has a short-term certificate program that teaches students how to become casino dealers. At the bigger and more luxurious casinos, dealers can make $100,000 or more.

And perhaps the most unusual two-year college of all—Deep Springs College, located on a cattle ranch and alfalfa farm near Death Valley, California, does education the way the ancient Greeks did it: small groups engaging in intensive study and thought, under the guidance of a professor. Many of its courses revolve around deep discussion rather than receiving information from on high. Some recent courses have included conservation science, Aristotle's *Ethics*, painting, mathematics in political life, and magical realism. Students at the two-year school are self-governing, and all students take part in some of the work of the farm, ranch, and college. That also makes it an idea place for people who like outdoors work and perhaps have interest in careers in farming or ranching.

Plus it's free, including room and board.

Deep Springs was the brainchild of an early tycoon in the electricity business, L. L. Nunn. He was interested in the teaching of ethics, and over time his philanthropic passions overtook his interest in electricity. He was especially interested in preparing generations of young people who would go forward to a "life in service of humanity."

•

Community college also can be a far less expensive route to some of the creative fields, such as becoming a chef, a makeup artist, or costume designer. Private trade schools in these fields generally cost a lot less than a four-year college or university, but even trade schools can be unaffordable for a lot of people. Community colleges are a much less expensive way to get started.

Susanna A. Song was drawn to painting and drawing as a kid, but as she was growing up in Southern California, her mother told her that art was a hobby, not a career. Her parents, who had immigrated from South Korea, didn't have the kind of money that would support what they considered impractical dreams.

"I knew I was a creative, but I didn't know where I wanted to go from there," Susanna said. "I liked the idea of fashion because my cousin was in the fashion industry in downtown LA. Maybe I'd go to a fashion school like Parsons. But my mom shot that down. I have no money, my family has no money, this is not a feasible action, and I figured I'd walk around aimlessly."

She took work at a law office but found it depressing sitting in a cubicle all day. "And so I thought, 'Let me go to community college and maybe I'll figure it out.'"

Community college in California costs less than $1,500 a year. And in a beginners' sewing class in Pasadena City College's division of fashion and costume design, Susanna found her way back to her dream of working in clothing design.

"I thought, *Wow, I could really get into this.*" While still in college, she began working for the Los Angeles fashion industry but found it a difficult place to make her way. At that time, LA's fashion industry was smaller, and companies were struggling.

Then a friend who was acting in a local drama production told Susanna that the costume designer for the play needed help. That ended up being her segue into costume design.

She was well trained at Pasadena City College, but she had no idea how to translate that into working for the entertainment industry, even though a huge portion of it is located in her backyard.

"I didn't have connections into Hollywood," she said. "But I posted on Craigslist that I would work for free for experience." Those unpaid gigs got her good recommendations and the opportunity to meet new people in the industry.

One job involved designing and sewing costumes for a music video. The costumes had to be created in multiples of three because the actors would get dunked in paint as part of the video. Susanna came to appreciate even more how well her community college courses had prepared her with the right skills in sewing and clothing construction.

"Over time, I made connections," Susanna said. "Friends who were producers or directors. I would do the work at a really low rate because it was a low-budget video. I kept saying yes to every job."

Finally, she landed a good job in an indie film with an $8 million budget. "I thought it was amazing. I had my own department with costumers. We shot in Russia, Romania, and Greece."

But when it became clear that the film wasn't going to do well or launch her into the business, she took a very short-term internship as an assistant to the president of the Costume Designers Guild. The job gave her membership in the union and access to a lot of people who could help.

Within a couple of days, she said, she made more connections than she'd made in all the time up to then.

Her supervisor at the union recommended her to someone who worked on the long-running ABC sitcom *The Goldbergs*, and that person brought her on to the show. At first, she was hired as an administrative assistant, but then she was offered a job in the wardrobe department. Within a year, she was hired to work as assistant costume designer for *Schooled*, a spinoff series to *The Goldbergs*. She was with the show for its only two seasons; it was canceled right before the COVID-19 pandemic.

Her best-known work, she said, was for the feature film *Minari*, about a family of Korean immigrants making a new life in Arkansas. It was a film that understandably had special meaning to her. She found out about the job through a producer and worked hard to get it, arguing that an Asian costume designer should be hired for such a movie. And she gave huge thought to the costuming: the way that older Koreans would hang on to their clothes through the years, disregarding fashion trends; the differences in the way such a family would dress in a large city as opposed to the rural South.

"I take my time with the script, and I really try to break it down, pulling references that inspire me," she said. "Things that might have been inspiring for the writer and director. The director already has a vision, but they also want more layers, and I love to create those layers. If I hadn't gotten into costumes, I would be a historian in some way."

Her work on the film became deeply personal as well.

"With all the research I had to do for the film, it was a life journey, kind of like a pilgrimage, working on *Minari*," Susanna told the publication *Awards Daily*. "Especially when I was looking at old photographs, thinking about all the dark secrets within a family, and why did a certain family member have to do that? When I read the script, it just gave me the perspective of my parents—the jobs that they had to take that they didn't like, and also the reasons why they did it."[1]

In 2021, *Minari* won both the Golden Globe and Sundance award for Best Foreign Language Film. It was nominated for an Oscar.

As much as Susanna loves to make connections and find more work, she also thinks it's important to be choosy when building a career in costume design.

"I turned down a lot of films that didn't seem right to me. After I hear back about how the film progressed, I find I did a good job by not taking it."

Costume design is among the lower-paid union jobs in the industry, she said. According to a union pay sheet, a costume designer in film who's on daily call makes more than $1,000 a day. It's a lot of daily income, but work in the entertainment industry is seldom every weekday, year-round.

Now in her late thirties, Susanna also is moving into new realms in the filmmaking world. She and her husband, who's already a writer/ director, have been working on a script about a North Korean boy.

She'd like to get a university education someday. She already has a lot of credits, and she cares about being an educated person. "I read the news. I try to educate myself every day."

But she finds that the lack of formal education hasn't held her back at all in her chosen work. Even though most of the designers listed in the union's directory have at least a bachelor's degree, it's not something the industry cares about seeing. "I've never been asked what was my highest education," Susanna said.

Far more important, she said, is knowing how to make connections, though she feels beginners shouldn't work for free the way she did. It's more about finding friends who are getting jobs and "attaching to their coattails." Building a presence on social media is also key; these days, Susanna said, a lot of designers are being contacted for work via Instagram.

And then the job requires working hard to be the kind of designer or member of the wardrobe staff who will be recommended to others.

"If you're young, give it all you've got," she said. "If you do a really good job, it will lead to another job right away."

•

There are a few four-year colleges that fit particularly well for people who find that a bachelor's degree might not be their best path *right now*. These schools have gotten the message about bringing more flexibility to higher education, including the idea that not all students need to pursue a bachelor's degree, or if they are and it's not working out, they should be able to drop back to an associate's degree.

Utah State University Eastern, less than two hours outside Salt Lake City, is a particularly promising model because of the variety of degrees and certificates it offers, and because, unlike at many four-year schools, those degrees aren't online. Online learning has its place, but research has shown that, depending on the course of study, students don't tend to learn as much. Those courses also leave students without the interaction that creates close relationships, which then become mentorships or friendships that help in future careers.

The Utah school also costs much less than most four-year schools, even for people who don't live in Utah—about $4,000 a year for residents and $11,000 for nonresidents—and accepts more than 90 percent of applicants.

It offers short-term certificates in more than forty fields as varied as 3D printing, environmental policy, web business, and practical nursing. Its associate's degree programs are more limited but include fields like agriculture, theater, and heavy machinery mechanics (for which average salaries start at more than $60,000 a year). Plus, it has a full range of bachelor's degree programs as well as a small graduate school.

So how is this better than attending a regular community college? A couple of ways. If you find yourself captivated by your studies and decide you want to go beyond an associate's degree and get a bachelor's, having the programs at one school, under one administration, makes it a much easier and smoother process. You might find that being at an affordable four-year school makes a bachelor's degree look more attractive, and if not, you still have an associate's degree to get your career going, unlike people who start out aiming for a bachelor's and then drop out without *any* degree or certificate.

In addition, you would begin your years as an upperclassman at a school where you've already made friends and are familiar with the campus and faculty. If you crave the traditional college-dorm experience, you can get that as a two-year student at USU Eastern—and dorm prices are incredibly low. In 2023, a small private room cost just $600 per semester, and the required meal plan of ten meals a week was less than $1,300.

We can expect (or at least hope) to see more of these kinds of flexible options as colleges start responding to what students actually need and can afford. Otherwise, any college that already has trouble attracting enough students might find itself in a fight for survival (more than fifty colleges have closed since 2016). Many colleges are no longer in a position to dictate precisely what kind of education students must have.

It might seem odd that a book about not getting a bachelor's degree should devote some words to a school that is mostly about offering exactly that. But the Evergreen State College in Olympia, Washington, is unique in ways that address the kinds of issues that keep many students out of college.

Professors at Evergreen don't give grades—students receive written evaluations instead—and rather than testing, base their evaluations on the skills and competencies the students have learned, as shown through their portfolios of work. Education at Evergreen is just as much about *doing* as it is about classroom learning. Students often design their own programs and areas of study.

The college also offers short-term certificate programs.

Evergreen is a state school, so for in-state residents the tuition is low, as is true of many state colleges. In this case, in 2023, the cost was $7,200 a year for in-state residents. But because of a reciprocal agreement with Oregon and California, the cost for students from those states was $10,419, much lower than most out-of-state tuition. Residents of other states pay a heftier $28,000, but that's still much less than most private schools, and Evergreen provides financial aid for many students.

It also offers some interesting other ways for reducing college costs.

The principal one and the one that first drew my interest: Evergreen honors work as a form of education. It gives college credit for the work and life experience of its students. That makes it ideal for readers of this book whose plan right after high school is to experience life, to find work or travel or public service or all three, and to find out more about themselves and the direction they want to take in life without or before college.

At Evergreen, those students take a special for-credit course that consists of thinking about and documenting their experiences and what they have learned from those. It's not a gut course; it involves real work. A professor guides each student through the process, which is also intended to help students think about what they have learned and gained from life so far, and where they want to take things next. At the same time, they can shorten their college time by a year or possibly more through the credit-for-work-experience.

For people who can't see spending four years of their life in classes, it's a dream solution. They can work independently, pondering and writing about their experiences rather than attend classes, and reduce the time and expense of attaining a bachelor's degree.

In addition to credit for work experience, students can earn many of their credits toward a degree through action rather than sitting and learning. Sam Stanton, the farmer featured in chapter 7, was able to finish the needed credits for his bachelor's at Evergreen by working on an ocean research vessel and journaling about what he was doing and learning.

Evergreen's certificate programs also come with college credits. The college is expanding the certificate program, which includes such fields as mycology (the study of mushrooms and yeasts), marine bioresources, drone mapping, marine fiber arts, managing nonprofits, climate policy, business finance, and sound postproduction for film and television.

Let's hope other colleges are sitting up and paying attention. Colleges that innovate might just change the public's viewpoint of how hard and expensive it is to get an education after high school.

CONCLUSION

Did you ever covet an MIT education but figure you wouldn't be one of the 5 percent of applicants to be accepted? Yeah, I wouldn't be either.

This isn't quite the same thing, but well over one thousand MIT courses are offered online by the great university via MIT OpenCourseWare. They're free, and they don't require applying, enrollment, or registration. Many but not all include lecture videos, and most include at least lecture notes as well as assignments (that you can decide to do or not). Some even have free online textbooks.

These MIT MOOCs (massive open online courses) are not just the engineering courses that make the university famous, though there are a couple hundred of those. MIT offers MOOCs in business (the Sloan School of Management is as well known as the university's tech offerings), history, architecture, anthropology, and literature. You can study French film classics, the human brain, classical music, or environmental science.

What you don't get: college credit or a grade. This is about learning for the pure pleasure and mental growth.

By now you know that there are many other ways to learn and live a good life without the formal classroom education of a four-year college. The lack of a bachelor's degree is not an excuse to be uneducated. In fact, as society and the work world shift more rapidly, it will be more important than ever to keep on learning.

This pertains to college graduates as well. Far too many of them don't bother learning that much during their years of supposedly higher education, and they stop learning altogether once they have a frameable baccalaureate certificate. The folks who keep on learning will put those other people in the shade over time.

Remember that employers are looking for "soft skills": The ability to learn quickly and the interest in doing so. Being engaged with the work and the organization. The willingness to work as a team member. People skills. Problem-solving. Enthusiasm and critical thinking. General knowledge about the world and current events are valued because those affect how the worlds of business, government, and the arts operate—not to mention their impact on your own life. All of this can be developed through an ongoing zest for learning.

There used to be two main routes for adults who wanted to learn: paid, in-person night school and the public library.

The library (and bookstores) are still great places to grow your mental abilities. Sadly, interest in reading for pleasure has been plummeting in the United States, according to a 2021 report by the National Assessment of Educational Progress. That's a shame because books aren't just a source of endless learning. Reading books activates the brain. Reading has been found to reduce stress and help you get to sleep. You go at your own pace and retain the material better than through watching or listening— even through excellent MIT MOOC lectures. Studies have shown that reading actually improves vocabulary, spelling, and math abilities. Even though reading might seem the opposite of social, it builds empathy and decision-making and social skills.

When my three kids were young, we would hold "family reading time" in the living room after dinner. Everyone read for an hour; even the preschooler would have picture books to go through. The interesting thing was that this hour ended up extending into "family discussion time," because, without our planning it at all, someone would have come across something in their book that got them thinking.

But then, I'm meeting you here on the page. You already know something about the value of books.

The internet, of course, now makes it easy to get the equivalent of a college education in other ways. Many universities offer MOOCs; Harvard also has a long list of courses, many practical, others just to stretch your mind. The list of schools goes on and on; just search for MOOC and the school you're interested in, or the subject. (I like searching by school because it brings up topics I never would have thought of on my own.) Just watch out for courses that charge money; there are a lot of them, often on the same sites as the free or low-cost ones.

Social media is another way to learn ideas and information, but it's one to use with caution. There's no real quality control, and the algorithms of sites like TikTok will sometimes push you further and further down a rabbit hole, toward certain groups with certain beliefs. You want to expand your mind, not prod it into dark corners where people present conspiracy theories and wild-eyed beliefs as facts.

At the same time, social media groups on Facebook and LinkedIn can be a great way to open your mind. When I was working on a story about snail farming in America, I joined a snail-enthusiast group on Facebook that kept me interested long after the article had been published. In order to find costume designers for this book, I joined a group of them on Facebook. Their immense love of fabrics and styles, the depth of their knowledge, and their desire to help each other have me hooked. I can't even sew—not yet, anyway—but I keep coming back to that group as they problem-solve together about antique textiles and the like.

The Khan Academy is free though mostly geared to the years before college, but it offers worthwhile courses in computers, storytelling, and other subjects that work for adults. And though MasterClass costs a little bit—$120 a year—and its "courses" are very short, I know people who swear by some of them, especially the ones that revolve around business and sales.

You probably already know that YouTube is a terrific source for practical instruction on just about anything. (Many MOOCs are on there as well.) A friend learned to crochet on YouTube. There are high-quality classes on videography, cooking, basic plumbing, health, and medicine. You get the idea.

Some organizations including Yale University offer free classes through Coursera, as well as low-cost courses leading to professional certificates. Coursera has some very expensive courses of study, but it's also the place where Google offers free and low-cost courses for certification that can be used to apply to the company with standing equal to that of a college grad.

In many states, community college classes are very low-cost or free, but in others can cost thousands of dollars a year. The in-person instruction makes them a great place for hands-on learning, such as studying a foreign language. Language skills can give you an extra boost in the workplace. Learning is often limited with virtual language classes—it helps to be able to interact in person with others in that particular tongue.

But don't just learn the knowledge you need for a specific job. True higher education, whether it's in a classroom or under your own design, means developing understanding of the world, critical thinking, and the mental plasticity to adapt and grow not just as a person who works, but as a person who can move more easily from one career to another, who takes part in this world, who enjoys engaging in it, and whose mind doesn't stultify from lack of exercise.

NOTES

Chapter 1

1. Pew Research Center, "10 Facts about Today's College Graduates," accessed April 12, 2024, https://www.pewresearch.org/short-reads/2022/04/12/10-facts-about-todays-college-graduates/
2. Public Agenda, "America's Hidden Common Ground on Public Higher Education: What's Wrong and How to Fix It," accessed from publicagenda.org. https://publicagenda.org/resource/americas-hidden-common-ground-on-public-higher-education-whats-wrong-and-how-to-fix-it/
3. Gallup, "Half Consider College Education Important," accessed from gallup.com. https://www.gallup.com/education/272228/half-consider-college-education-important.aspx
4. *Los Angeles Times* Editorial Board, "Reimagine California Education," *Los Angeles Times*, June 6, 2021, https://www.latimes.com/opinion/story/2021-06-06/editorial-reimagine-california-education
5. The *New York Times* Editorial Board, "Why Do So Many Employers Require College Degrees?" *New York Times*, October 18, 2021, https://www.nytimes.com/2021/10/18/opinion/college-degrees-employers.html
6. The *Washington Post* Editorial Board, "Why Do So Many Employers Require a College Degree?" The *Washington Post*, July 20, 2021, https://

www.washingtonpost.com/opinions/2021/07/20/majority-americans-lack
-college-degree-why-do-so-many-employers-require-one/

7. Harvard Business School, "Dismissed by Degrees," accessed from hbs.edu,
https://www.hbs.edu/managing-the-future-of-work/Documents/dismissed
-by-degrees.pdf

8. ProCon.org, "Is a College Education Worth It?" accessed from college
-education.procon.org, https://college-education.procon.org/

9. Research.com, "Percentage of High School Graduates That Go to
College," accessed from research.com, https://research.com/education
/percentage-of-high-school-graduates-that-go-to-college

Chapter 3

1. AmeriCorps, "State of the Evidence Report 2017," accessed from
americorps.gov, https://americorps.gov/sites/default/files
/evidenceexchange/FR_2017%20State%20of%20the%20Evidence
%20Report_1.pdf

2. Deloitte, "2018 Deloitte Impact Survey," accessed from deloitte.com,
https://www2.deloitte.com/content/dam/Deloitte/us/Documents/us
-deloitte-impact-survey.pdf

3. Reading Partners, "AmeriCorps Living Stipend," accessed from
readingpartners.org. https://readingpartners.org/blog/americorps-stipend
-living/

Chapter 4

1. IBM, "IBM Apprenticeship," accessed from ibm.com, https://www.ibm
.com/impact/feature/apprenticeship

Chapter 5

1. University of Pennsylvania Wharton School, "Can You Run a Business
Without Going to Business School?" accessed from online.wharton
.upenn.edu, https://online.wharton.upenn.edu/blog/can-you-run-a
-business-without-going-to-business-school/

2. MIT Sloan Executive Education, "The Truth About Entrepreneurship:
6 Myths Debunked," accessed from exec.mit.edu, https://exec.mit.edu/s
/blog-post/the-truth-about-entrepreneurship-6-myths-debunked
-MCYH7OP7FLIVA5PJD5FO6TY7MC5I

3. US Chamber of Commerce, "State of Small Business Now," accessed

from uschamber.com, https://www.uschamber.com/small-business/state-of-small-business-now

4. SmallBizGenius, "Crowdfunding Statistics," accessed from smallbizgenius.net, https://www.smallbizgenius.net/by-the-numbers/crowdfunding-stats/tha

Chapter 10

1. Harvard Business School, "The Emerging Degree Reset," accessed from hbs.edu, https://www.hbs.edu/managing-the-future-of-work/Documents/research/emerging_degree_reset_020922.pdf

2. Bureau of Labor Statistics, "Projections Overview and Highlights, 2021-31," accessed from bls.gov, https://www.bls.gov/opub/mlr/2022/article/projections-overview-and-highlights-2021-31.htm

Chapter 11

1. Associated Press, "US Military Wrestles with Rising Racism, Discrimination," accessed from apnews.com, https://apnews.com/article/us-military-racism-discrimination-4e840e0acc7ef07fd635a312d9375413

Chapter 12

1. Awards Daily, "Minari Costume Designer Susanna Song on Reflecting Culture Through Clothing," accessed from awardsdaily.com. https://www.awardsdaily.com/2021/02/18/minari-costume-designer-susanna-song-on-reflecting-culture-through-clothing/

ACKNOWLEDGMENTS

This book is a guide to thriving without a bachelor's degree, told through the best guides in the world: the people who have done it, lived it, and had the phenomenal generosity to tell their honest stories. They wanted not only to give you, the reader, the benefit of their experiences, triumphs, and advice, but also to share their vulnerabilities and the moments that didn't work out so well. That is not an easy job, but they all did it with a great self-reflection and caring.

Some are making a lot of money, and some aren't. That's not what matters. They all are courageous people who went against the grain to create lives that feel authentic to them and bring them pride, and they are giving you the best of what they have learned on the journey. I'm deeply grateful to them all.

My agent, Katherine Cowles, took me through the process with phenomenal expertise and hasn't steered me wrong once. She is a true advocate. I especially appreciate her commitment to quality work—solid reporting and excellent writing. Thanks also to editor Alexis Lipsitz for getting me through the early iterations. Former HarperCollins editor Andrea Fleck-Nisbit was across the country having the same thoughts I was about the role of college in our society, and the book never would have happened if she hadn't already known that families needed it. Austin Ross was the HarperCollins editor who saw it through to conclusion and made the process more painless than I thought possible. Thanks also for solving a couple of thorny problems with great creativity.

Research assistant Katie Waddell was a tremendous help in finding some of the sources for the book. I'm also grateful that the process of creating the book made my life intersect with that of fellow writer and life warrior Anna Goodman Herrick.

Thanks to my editors at the *Los Angeles Times* for backing my work and granting me a book leave.

Friends, family, and colleagues were tolerant and helpful observers, cheerleaders, and sometimes necessary critics. Jordan Hiltner especially could always be counted on to bring laughter and unicorns into every day. And special thanks to my wonderful partner, Rick Shaine, who supported me in taking on this project even though he knew it would absorb time and energy in our life. He listened to my endless chatter about the latest interviews or data, offered canny observations, and made sure that at the end of particularly tiring days, I had adequate take-out dinners. The Cajun food was particularly appreciated.

ABOUT THE AUTHOR

Karin Klein is an award-winning journalist who has spent most of her career as an editorial writer at the *Los Angeles Times*, covering education, medicine, science, and the environment. She has been awarded numerous fellowships, from the 2006 Pulliam Fellowship for Editorial Writers to the 2024 fellowship of the Institute for Citizens and Scholars for reporting on career and technical education. She recently returned to school part-time to study archaeology at Palomar College in San Diego County.

She is a graduate of Wellesley College and attended UC Berkeley journalism school but never completed her master's degree because she found her newspaper job first. (Skills before degrees.)

Klein is a certified naturalist with OC Parks and the American Cetacean Society, and the author of the interpretive nature guide *50 Hikes in Orange County*, now in its second edition. When not writing, reading, cooking new dishes, or practicing piano, she's most likely to be found on hiking trails.

She lives in Laguna Beach, California, with her partner, film editor Rick Shaine, their two dogs, and Tim the Cat.